RAISED!

An inspirational story of two courageous young parents
in the midst of a tragic accident and the love, grace,
and miracles that save three lives.

Margaret J. Cotton

As told by

Charlie and Florentina Mada

ISBN 978-1-64258-123-2 (paperback)
ISBN 978-1-64258-124-9 (digital)

Christian Faith Publishing, Inc.
832 Park Avenue
Meadville, PA 16335
www.christianfaithpublishing.com

Printed in the United States of America

PRAISE FOR RAISED!

This book may change what you believe. A gripping story of a couple who saw their only child snatched away in the blink of an eye. Your own heart will be broken, then repaired as you read this detailed account of how a mother's love, hope and faith brought forth a story of ultimate survival. Raised is a must-read for anyone who has suffered loss or is entering into such a time. Never lose faith, cling to hope and experience overwhelming love: you will find this message in Raised.

Ralph Dettman

In a world filled with violence and death, this riveting account of new life for a Romanian family provides a remarkable and inspiring story needing to be told! This incredible, faith-building biography of God's miraculous intervention in the wake of devastating tragedy is one that will capture people's hearts and catalyze their faith. The fascinating details of a dramatic incident and amazing outcome will challenge anyone's attempt to put an expiration date on hope.

Dr. Dale Whilden, President of Ocean Grove Camp Meeting Association

A must book to read! "Raised!" is the story of an unbelievable journey to faith of a family! It is how God can touch someone's life in completely unexpected ways and radically transform it through the miracle of salvation. The story is told artfully, with great attention to detail. It is an complex journey with many challenges for Charlie and Flori, but they all fit together perfectly in a plan that only God can put together and only He is able to make it happen.

Cristian Ianculovici

Excellent for Book Clubs and Small Groups
Judy Fury at Manasquan Presbyterian Church (NJ)

This book is almost impossible to put down. The reader is compelled to keep in step with the Madas as they traverse all the obstacles in their lives. This is a book that offers a renewal of belief in a higher power and provides a platform for anyone who may be facing a crisis in their lives. The author's style is colorful, dramatic and precise. The details of accounts make you feel that you are actually there. The feeling of hope and fortitude is woven throughout the manuscript. A true story of inspiration and hope! A message to everyone that miracles do happen.

Dr. Allan Lifson, MFCC /University Professor Costa Mesa, CA

A book that I think will have an impact in many lives by its challenging message. I am delighted to write these words and hopeful that God will perform miracles in many families and many lives passing through trial and who need support, comfort and liberation. Humbly, I pray that God will use the testimony of the Mada family so that in the end the Lord Jesus be glorified and exalted in many hearts. I embrace and bless those who made it possible to be written and those who will read the book "Raised!"

Mihai Sarbu-Irimia, New Life Romanian Church, Glendale AZ

What a great book! From the first page to the last, the reader gets deeply immersed into this beautiful, fascinating, filled with God's interventions story of the Mada family. Their story is God's story and I am so glad that they are sharing it with the world. After reading the book, you will feel motivated, challenged, strengthened in your faith and reminded that *Jesus Christ is the same yesterday, today, and forever,* and *with God all things are possible.* This is a must-read book for people from all walks of life; from those struggling with faith, to those who are mature in faith.

John Todor Pastor, First Baptist Church of Kasson, MN

I have read the Raised manuscript, and it was certainly a blessing to me. As their pastor for a number of years, I know that Charlie and Flori are remarkable people and the journey that God used to win them to Himself is both remarkable and miraculous. Their journey to America and all God has done in their lives should bring hope and blessings to all that share it with them as they read a real-life miracle "Raised"!

Jim B Taylor, Pastor

Raised is a story of hope and resurrection. Raised, which shares the miraculous revival of a young child, spreads the Good News of Jesus Christ as Savior. In today's fast-paced society, Raised's message of faith may inspire readers to step back and explore their own relationship with Christ.

Andrea Jo Rodgers, Author, At Heaven's Edge: True Stories of Faith and Rescue

In Raised, the Madas tell how God drew them to himself in extraordinary ways. Charlie's willingness to follow God's mysterious leading, and Florentina's willingness to put aside her doubts and follow Charlie led them to the place of faith and obedience where they continue to reside today.

Jeanette F. Chaplin, Ed.D. Author of Flowers of the Field mystery series

I can hardly wait for the movie!

Faith Jones

Dedicated to the glory of God through Jesus Christ

And in thanksgiving for his love for Marius and Caroline

Everything is a miracle.

—Albert Einstein

"When John, who was in prison, heard about the deeds of the Messiah, he sent his disciples to ask him, "Are you the one who is to come, or should we expect someone else?" Jesus replied, "Go back and report to John what you hear and see: The blind receive sight, the lame walk, those who have leprosy are cleansed, the deaf hear, the dead are raised, and the good news is proclaimed to the poor."

—Matthew 11:2-5, NIV

INTRODUCTION

Ocean Grove, NJ
March 25, 2015, 9:08 p.m.

THE STORY I AM GOING to share with you is one of the most compelling and amazing stories of life and death I have ever heard. It is a story of extreme anguish followed by a powerful series of miracles and divine interventions. A miracle, by definition, requires faith to see and believe. So this book will challenge faith. The Mada's story may even create more questions than answers, because it is not a story of merit, but of grace.

I write it tonight surrounded by our family's equally anguished tears and prayers for a friend's child. Caroline is a new teenage driver, and she is fighting for her life this very moment in a New Jersey emergency room. Her parents are in the grip of grief. In both fear and faith, our community prays for a miracle to sustain and bless her life. Tonight, we remember that despair is a powerful and demanding companion.

The story you are about to read is a strong reminder that, in God, we have an even greater and ever-present comforter. If we are ever to experience any peace in understanding why, when, and to whom miraculous healing is anointed, it is not likely to be here on earth. And yet I believe we have a compassionate, just, and loving God.

This is the story Charlie and Flori tell. It is seared into their conscience, and they experience it in the present tense. There are witnesses that swear this is what they saw happen. There are government documents that declare it so. I believed them before I saw that proof. In that faith, I offer this story to you as a true witness.

Margaret J. Cotton

CHAPTER 1

Phoenix, Arizona
December 1995
Flori

"MOM, CAN WE TALK ABOUT the accident I went through?"

I look in the mirror to the back seat at our son, Marius, as he is pushing a Hot Wheels car over the contours of his pudgy legs. He has become a sports car speedway, banking on the knee curves and racing down the shin straightaway.

"What would you like me to tell you about the accident?"

I am surprised at Marius's question. All days are considered either "before" or "after" the day of his accident, but it was not something we discussed. Although Charlie and I have spoken in general terms with people in our church about the accident, we have never shared all the details of Marius's miracle in front of him. He is young; there is time, and he has never asked. Curious about what details he wants me to explain, I ask again, "What do you want me to tell you?"

Marius stops playing with the car and intensely looks at me. "I would like to tell you when I wasn't with you guys, you guys shouldn't have called me back."

"Back from where?"

"I was in Heaven with My Lord, and I didn't want to come back. You guys cried and called me back, and Lord sent me back for you guys." Marius's voice is direct and emphatic, and he stops playing with the car to look at me.

Marius's totally serious attitude has left me weak and speechless. I have avoided thinking of the dark terror that Marius must have experienced in those last few minutes. I never considered that he was with God. I check the traffic on East I-10, take a deep breath, and ask, "How does the Lord look?"

"Beautiful."

I wait, but Marius doesn't add any details, so I repeat, "How does Lord look?"

"Beautiful."

"Beautiful and how else?"

"Beautiful, beautiful! Can't tell you more than just that. All I want to tell you is that if this ever happens again, please don't call crying for me again because I don't want to come back."

How could Marius be telling me these things? I look in the rearview mirror again and ask, "Do you ever think this will happen again?"

"I don't know, but I just don't want you guys to call me back anymore." Marius begins to play with the toy car again. The traffic on East I-10 is flowing smoothly toward Phoenix. Although my eyes are on the road, my mind is racing, trying to process what my son has said. In that instant, I have a vision—if not in my eyes, then in my heart. A man's long, white robe fills the sky. His face glows, and it is so radiant, I cannot see his nose or eyes or mouth. I see Marius, holding tightly to a leg defined beneath the robe. Gently, in a gesture of loving encouragement, the man's two hands push Marius toward me. An outpouring of love, acceptance, peace, joy, and beauty fills me. The vision lasts an instant, but I completely understand its importance and its reality. I haven't any questions. I easily accept the truth of all Marius has said. As soon as I do, something indescribable is released. And although there is something profoundly absent, joy remains in my heart.

In some unexplainable way, I am transformed. Within that vision, the entire horrific ordeal takes a universal shift. Charlie and I had a completely different experience from Marius! We had experienced all parents' worst fears and pain. But at the worst possible moment of Marius's young life, he had been in the full embrace of the love of the Lord. It is a place so beautiful, he hadn't wanted to return to us.

Later, warmed by the early evening desert sun, I wait in our backyard for Charlie to come home. I am thinking about how I will share the extraordinary request our son made in the car. Charlie is a little late, and I begin remembering the day Marius's story began almost five years earlier. I shudder as I imagine the precise, tragic moment from which an arrow went forth, piercing and realigning every aspect of our lives: our self-images, marriage, careers, finances, citizenship, culture, language, values, faith, and even our eternity. It has been a long journey, but miraculously, we finally made it to the same place—the full embrace of the love of our Lord Jesus.

CHAPTER 2

~~~~·o·c\·c·ro·6·r·o·/·o·o·m~~~~

Pelican Resort, Danube Delta, Romania
Tuesday, August 6, 1991
Flori

SOFT MORNING LIGHT FILTERS THROUGH the sheer, long curtains that
are stirred by the breeze. Beyond the occasionally billowing curtains
lie a covered patio, lawn, and then the Danube. With my eyes closed,
I can hear the rustling sound of the reeds on the riverbank, and smell
the exquisite scents of the Delta flowers. Marius, our sixteen-month-
old son, lies between Charlie and me. He isn't wiggling around trying
to get down and explore with his usual curious energy.

A slow, soft morning. This is a young mother's paradise, and the
day one only dreams of enjoying. I smile at the sweet luxury of the
time spreading ahead of us on this vacation. I stretch and take a deep
breath, pointing my toes and arching my back. The sheets are like
silk, and I am in Heaven.

Within a few moments, Marius rolls over and touches my face
with his fingers, his cute little fingers, my son's fingers. I will never
tire of being filled with an immense wonder of him. I softly touch
his nose. He smiles back and traces my nose, and my lips, and then
reaches for my necklace. He does this often; it is part of our private routine. Charlie opens his eyes and smiles at me over Marius's
head. He makes a loud, funny snoring sound and closes his eyes
again. Marius rolls over to his father and traces the lines of Charlie's
lips, laughing at Charlie's morning stubble. Charlie pretends to snore
again, and Marius collapses into a belly laugh. Laughing at the noth-

12

ingness of such a silly moment only makes it all the funnier and worthy of more squeals and giggles.

Marius rolls back and forth between us, exploring variations of the game. I pretend I am asleep, and Marius's kiss wakes me. We all laugh. Charlie pretends to be asleep and snore. Marius grabs his nose, and we all laugh. It was unusual for the baby to linger more than a few minutes at any game. But this morning it is different, so the game goes on and on. These moments of tender love are so much more than just being relaxed. Charlie seems unusually content. He hasn't even mentioned his fishing plans. I can see this magic of being a family is also filling him. There was nothing more important, nowhere else to be.

Charlie tickles Marius; Marius tickles me. We ruffle his hair, tickle his toes, and noisily blow rude sounds into his belly. Marius gives us juicy, open-mouthed, baby kisses, leaving drool running down our cheeks. And it is all wonderful. Marius doesn't tire of our game, even after he becomes too tired to laugh. He quiets down and begins to use just his leg to touch first Charlie then me. And when he tires of that, he slowly reaches out with his right arm and hand, touching one and then the other. As Marius's eyes begin to close, his little arm and hand just seem to float above his head, defying gravity. Charlie reaches up and gently grasps our little boy's fingers, bringing his arm down to rest on his small body.

"Our son is getting stronger!" he beams.

"Yes, he is strong like his daddy," I say. Charlie smiles back.

The effort slows down to a dream-ballet. It goes on and on until Marius, who no longer takes morning naps, just closes his eyes and falls asleep. Marius stirs twice, reaching out to see if I am near. I touch his cheek and pat his hand, and he falls back to sleep. Watching him sleep is all we want to do. His fingers, his eyes, a small curl in his hair, the long eyelashes are perfect. How is it the love of someone so young can complete—and increase—our love for each other?

Charlie also drifts back to a gentle sleep, and I drift off to sweet memories. Sixteen months earlier, we had received a phone call to come to the hospital and meet our son. We had wanted to be parents for eight years, and this phone call ended a painful journey.

The nurse had brought out the blanket-bound, tiny baby and placed him in my arms. And just at that moment when the baby looked up into my eyes, nearby church bells had begun to ring out a beautiful hymn. It was loud and had startled everyone. The bell's echoing peals gave me warm chills, and I brought my face down close to the baby, breathing his breath. We all cried. The hymn continued, and the nurse and Charlie and I agreed it was surely a sign of a rich blessing on the adoption.

I still have chills when I look into his adorable face. I never tire of whispering, "You are my son, and I am your mother!" I want to be lost in this joy and linger in the soft, golden light still filling the room. I marvel that in such precious moments, we continue to be woven into a family until, unexpectedly, I am startled as if waking for the first time in an unfamiliar hotel room. Marius's long, dark eyelashes are still closed in sweet sleep. Charlie is awake, but he hasn't moved. We smile, and our fingers touch and entwine across our sleeping child.

I don't need anything else. I have a good husband. We are rich. I have a son. We are happy. I need nothing else. I have everything.

I think, *We have everything, Charlie. There is nothing more I need or want.*

I don't know, but now I wonder if perhaps with those words, the morning's magic was gone, and the darkness began its approach. All the suffering that unfolded from that morning we consider just birthing pains to a greater light.

CHAPTER 3

Murighiol, Romania
Tuesday, August 6, 1991, about noon
Charlie

FLORI IS KEEPING HER EYE on Marius as he toddles around the hotel room, exploring the nooks and crannies of the suite.

"Let's go outside and explore this amazing place," I say, hoping to spend as little time in our room as possible.

My wife agrees, and we walk outside our room onto a covered porch. Flori was born to be a mother, and she takes the job very seriously. Marius is never more than an arm's length from her, picking up bits of twigs and little stones. Our son is very curious and smart. Maybe Flori has taught him to be that way. He imitates the birds hopping from branch to branch above his head. He jumps up with little toe-hops, attempting to join the birds in the trees. I am delighted when he sings to them in his baby-babble. I take him by the hand, and we walk over to the river edge. He is great, and I love being his father.

"The river is full of carp and bluegills. They say all you need to do is throw in the line and the fish jump onto the hook! Look at the rich, blue water!" I rub my hands in anticipation, and Marius laughs and rubs his hands together with me. "The booklet said the restaurant cleans and cooks the fish you will catch." I flash my most winsome smile and wink at Flori.

"Tomorrow we are going to eat lots of fish, Marius!" Flori laughs. She understands that I want to go fishing this afternoon.

"I am getting hungry. Since I have not caught a big fish, and the restaurant is closed today, let's go into town."

"Sure, that sounds very good." Flori goes back into our room and gathers an extra sweater and other items for the baby.

I can remember the route from several years ago when just Flori and I had visited for a shorter stay. Trees along the road's edge create dark, leafy tunnels. It is easy to drive to a nearby rustic, but charming village. The restaurant, although not pretentious, provides a pleasant lunch. Marius is coy with the waiter, playing peek-a-boo with his napkin.

"Oh, he is a cute one," the waiter laughs.

Flori smiles. Marius seems more intent to be the center of attention than to eat his sandwich. It seems all too natural for everyone to stop by our table and tell us how adorable he is. That is the way it is with Marius; he makes friends with everyone, no matter what age they are. Once we finish our meal, Marius wants to climb the tree outside the restaurant's double doors. I hold his two hands and help him balance and walk out on the lower limb. I am surprised by his courage. He is not afraid. Another boy joins Marius in the tree. He is older, and Marius is thrilled just to watch him scramble up to the highest branch.

"Next year, Marius. Next year you will be old enough to climb so high."

I try to lift him from the lower limb, but he grabs on tighter and ends up hanging and swinging from it. He makes me laugh. "You are a little monkey!" I know he doesn't know what a monkey is, but my son giggles and drops to the ground. I think, *He is growing. He will be a strong, young man someday.*

Flori is talking with another family who has bought a huge cantaloupe from a nearby street market. They explain the rich, Delta soil grows fruit twice the size of that sold anywhere else. It looks ripe and sweet.

"Flori, let's go buy one while we are here," I offer. It seems like such an ordinary decision now. How innocent to suggest to stop. The walk is pleasant, and the market is as colorful as we had been told. We do not rush since we have nothing to do all afternoon.

"Good day, sir," Flori greets a farmer standing behind a table filled with beautiful fruit and vegetables. "You have amazing fruit!" The elderly man smiles at my pretty wife and thanks her for her kindness. I am pleased when I see Flori talk with strangers so comfortably.

"Would you like to taste the vegetables?" he asks.

"Yes! But today I will buy only this cantaloupe." Flori picks up the fruit and smells its ripeness.

"Well, tomorrow come back, and I will sell you melons and vegetables!" They all laugh as I carry it back to the car under my arm.

"Oh, Flori. I can smell how sweet it is going to taste. I have my pocketknife. Let's find a sunny place with a nice view on the way back to the resort. We can just relax, set up our chairs, and eat it." So it is my idea to drive and stop at a scenic route along the river's edge.

Soon the natural environment of open, grassy areas provides expansive views of the water. The two-lane road curves and meanders over the small hills. Small, white and blue wildflowers fearlessly grow with the grasses next to the road. Occasionally, clusters of large blossoms of bright orange and yellow flowers accent a curve. We see one lovely view and then another. Flori is wearing a scarf to protect her curls from the wind, and the ends of the scarf gracefully dance around her face. She catches the ends and twirls them around her finger. The world looks big and beautiful and kind.

About 2:30, I pull into an area where the road's shoulder is wider and provides a safe area to park. A large lake is especially close to the road, and nearby, a few campers are setting up several tents and folding chairs. And although Flori smiles and tells me it is perfect and just where she had hoped we would stop, I am the one who stops and parks the car here, at this place. I am the one who decides.

CHAPTER 4

Beside the road from Murighiol to Tulcea
August 6, 1991, about 2:35 p.m.
Charlie

WHEN THE CAR DOOR SLAMS, a large flock of white pelicans takes flight. Flori points and says, "Look! Look, Marius! Look at all the birds!" The pelicans soar in a formation and then land in the lake's gentle current. "Let's go see the birdies, Marius."

I bring out a collapsible picnic table. I carefully arrange the new comfortable chairs in such a way that we can have the best view of the landscape. There is a smaller one for Marius between ours. Marius has lost interest in the birds, which are now only floating on the water, and he has begun hunting for sticks. Flori and I slowly return to the chairs.

Flori picks up the cantaloupe. "I'll cut it. You go ahead and play with Marius." While she begins to prepare the melon, cutting the sweet orange flesh into bite-sized pieces, I play tag with Marius. I run past the table a few times, stealing cantaloupe pieces. She laughs and pops melon pieces into Marius's and her mouths. I point and tease her that I caught her eating also. She smiles and tempts me to taste a bite. "It is as juicy as he promised!"

I return to sit down in the folding chair to enjoy the fruit. "Marius is finding even the twigs very interesting. He no longer wants to play tag," I complain. But my smile gives me away that I am again teasing and happy to sit down and eat more melon. Music begins to play, and I notice for the first time the extent of the nearby

18

campsite. The music sounds as if it is a radio. Flori is also listening and nods her head to the lively tune.

Flori hands me several slices. "It is very good, Charlie." With the temperature in the mid-seventies, and a warm breeze gently keeping flies away, there is nothing to do but be content. I put my feet up and close my eyes. Flori sits down facing me, as the warmth of the sun washes over my face.

"This is so juicy. I am glad we bought one. Maybe we should have gotten one for tomorrow too," Flori sighs.

"We can go back tomorrow and buy another one and vegetables!" I laugh.

"Can you see Marius?" Flori is looking around, with her hand blocking the sun.

"Yes, he is now playing peek-a-boo again." I cheer him on with clapping and laughing.

Flori swipes a few stray ants from her leg. "Oh, he knows he is the cleverest boy to make his daddy smile and laugh."

Marius runs over and carefully tags my arm. Then he runs a few steps and looks back, inviting me to chase him. "Your son knows how to get me up!" I pretend I cannot catch him, falling and rolling on the ground. Marius jumps on my stomach, and we wrestle with tickling and laughter. Finally, I grab Marius and lift him over my shoulder.

It doesn't seem like Flori tires of watching me play with Marius. She cheers when Marius avoids my exaggerated attempts to capture him. We dart from behind her, to the left and then to the right. I then charge and grab Marius again, swinging him up and over my head. Fifty feet behind Flori's back I spot a pipe, about two-and-a-half feet in diameter and four feet tall. It sits on a raised, concrete foundation that has a four-inch ledge. I carry Marius over to look at it more closely. I put Marius down to inspect the top, which is sealed with a metal lid that had been welded in place. It is tightly sealed, and Marius begins running around the pipe. We chase each other around the pipe.

"It is nice to see the two of you boys enjoying yourselves. I get to play at the playground each day. This is boys' play, large and full of running. I am going to put my feet up and just relax!"

"Good idea! I will relax too!" Surprisingly tired, I sit back down with a sigh. We chat about how nice the hotel is and about my anticipation of fishing success. Flori tells me that every day, Marius has the same effect as I saw this morning, making friends of strangers.

"Would you like to see the ruins of Halmyris, tomorrow?" I ask, hoping that she will insist I go fishing.

"Let's see what the weather is like." Flori smiles and offers another ripe piece of orange melon.

"Well, I can fish in any weather," I hint. "There is no hurry. We can go sightseeing later in the week."

"I saw photographs of ponds with huge, floating lilies. That would be nice." I am not sure if she is teasing me, so I give her a playful wink.

"We have so much time," she laughs and claps for Marius, who is hop-jumping with two feet. Each time he lands without falling, he looks to see if his skill is being admired.

I smile. "Yes, lots. Here, Marius, come sit in your chair. I have fixed it for you."

Marius runs over and starts climbing into the chair.

"No, no. Here, let me show you." Getting his attention, I get up and then sit down slowly in my own chair. Immediately Marius tries to climb over the arm, upsetting the whole thing and landing on the ground. It is true, I am annoyed. I do not have Flori's patience.

Flori tries to get him to sit in the chair, but just as she gets him into a good position, Marius quickly brings up his feet and stands on the seat.

"He thinks it is another game, Charlie."

So we work together and carefully put him into the chair, but Marius stands up again, only to have the chair tip over. Marius fusses just enough to express disappointment in the chair's lack of cooperation. I want to sit down and relax, so I close up the little chair and lean it against the table. Undaunted, Marius is up and running again, back and forth behind the pipe, peeking out on each side. I had expected him to make more of a fuss when I closed the chair, but he is content with his new game. I don't mind because I can play it while sitting down. Each time he peeks out, I point and call out that I can see him.

Flori finishes her list of vacation possibilities by saying, "Well, we have many choices. All things are possible, but nothing is necessary!" I am especially enjoying how relaxed Flori is now. She often hovers at our son's side, not letting him out of reach. But Marius is getting older, and she is sitting here enjoying my company.

I nod toward Marius. "He is so clever. He finds something to do and enjoy in the simplest of things." Flori can see Marius walking around the pipe's raised concrete foundation. One foot is on the concrete four-inch ledge; the other is on the grass. Off balance, Marius wobbles.

"Charlie, he makes my most ordinary days most extraordinary. He helps me remember to enjoy the tiniest things that I might overlook."

I smile and reach over and pat her hand. She places her hand over mine, and I see her wedding band. I remember our wedding day. It was a great day, but this is even a better one. The deep colors of the Danube's expansive grassland intensify the contentment that washes over us. Near the pipe, Marius sings a soft, unrecognizable song as he climbs onto its concrete ledge, and then jumps off onto the ground. A few times he stumbles and falls, but soon he is able to land confidently on two feet with his arms triumphantly raised. It is quiet, except for the birds hidden in the grasses and the distant radio tunes. The sun ducks behind a cloud or two. It is too quiet.

"Can you see him?" Flori asks with a sudden urgency.

"Yes, yes. I can see him." I wave my hand toward the pipe. "Has your constant vigilance returned?"

I am aware that Flori is watching my eyes search for our son. In the distance, there is a very small sandy beach, and the lake's edge is lined with reeds. Everything is still; I can no longer see Marius. Our boy has been walking behind the four-foot high pipe, so I have been able to see him first on the left and then the right. His arm, his hair, and his chubby little legs were visible every few seconds. But now I do not see him.

Flori is watching me scanning the area, and without my smile or a look of relief, her concerns increase. She demands, "Can you really see him?"

I do not answer. I cannot see him in the grass behind the pipe. I am certain Marius has not wandered off. He might have found some little caterpillar or stone to inspect behind the pipe. I do not answer Flori because I am certain I will see him any second. It hasn't been long enough to justify her tone.

"Can you actually see him?" she shouts.

I am annoyed, so I interrupt her. "Relax. Look where we are!" I wave to the grass. "If you cannot relax here, then where and when will you relax?" I try not to show my annoyance, and I give Flori a small smile. "It is beautiful here. I am watching. You need to relax. You will suffocate him." She does not return my smile, but instead twists around in her chair to see for herself.

"He is behind the pipe?" she asks, looking at me with a distrust that shakes me deeply. "There is something wrong. I know! I just know! If you don't get up and find him, I will." Flori sits forward and begins to stand up.

The sun goes behind a cloud, and the shadow is cold and unnerving. I am startled by how quickly the cold penetrates my heart, like the coldness of Flori's implied accusations.

"Will you take a break?" I stand up and push her back into the chair. It is harder than I intend, and Flori falls back into the chair. Flori is overreacting, and I turn and head toward the pipe to end her unnecessary panic. While walking a dozen steps back toward the pipe, I wonder how suddenly our peaceful and happy moment has dissolved into Flori's sometimes-compulsive care and control. As a man, I know Marius needs to grow into a curious and confident man himself. I shake my head, thinking about how can I convince Flori to allow Marius to develop a healthy independence. First, I need to spot Marius and bring him back to her quickly to demonstrate her baseless fear.

Within a few steps, I am confused. I can now see more of the grassy area where I had expected to see Marius crouching and digging with his stick. Instead, the entire area is empty. The empty spaces and my concern explode in my chest. I reach the very back of the pipe and walk around, thinking perhaps Marius is very good at playing a game of hide and seek. *Is he staying out of sight on purpose?* I look back at Flori, who would have seen Marius come around the pipe, if that was Marius's new game.

Flori's expression is one of deepening concern. She clearly has not spotted our son. I search again around the back of the pipe, but our son is not there. Next, I look toward the water, but it is too far away. The baby couldn't have walked that far without coming into my line of sight. The slight slope toward the edge of the lake is short grass, nowhere for a small boy to hide. I run toward the bank, but the time it takes me to run just a fraction of the distance convinces me that Marius has not reached the reeds.

"How can this be? Children don't just disappear," I mumble to no one. Frantically looking in every direction, I realize there is nothing to see. I just saw my son, and there hasn't been time for him to wander away. My son's disappearance is impossible. The breeze shifts slightly, and the melody of a popular song drifts louder from the campers. They have several picnic tables up and have created a little circle of canvas tents and tarps. Marius loves music and enjoys playing with the buttons and dials of our stereo at home. I am forced to consider other explanations. *Did Marius have time to run over there? Could he have run over to them and charmed the people there? Had his smile made its way into the family circle? Had there been that much time?* It seems impossible.

I look back at the tall pipe and see something new. A few inches from the large pipe's foundation is a small, bare spot in the grass. I decide the bare spot is nothing—until I take a step closer and understand it is not just a hole. It is a second pipe—a small, gray, plastic pipe. The top of the pipe has been roughly cut off at ground level with a small amount of concrete unevenly surrounding it. Uncut grass hides its edges, but it is way too small to be a danger. I try to move the larger pipe's lid and am convinced it is still securely sealed. When I look again at the smaller pipe, I see a tiny, green frog and twigs floating on the surface of the shallow water. No, it is too small. The music from the tents starts up again, and I look toward the group of green canvas tents where a few adults are standing around and talking.

"Maybe he is there!" I call to Flori, but she isn't looking and probably doesn't hear me.

I hear Flori's screams, which are now hysterical. She is pacing, holding her head with her hands. It makes my entire body cramp just to see her in such distress. But it is impossible for our baby to be in the small, shallow pipe. I need to find Marius in the camp. I will carry our giggling son back to his mother and end this. All of this will all be over within a few minutes. If he is there, I will lift my son onto my shoulders and march back to Flori. She will stop screaming and smile and then laugh. My best hope is the campsite, so I do not look back, and I race across the field.

But the campers at the tents have heard her agonizing scream, and several walk from behind the tents to see what is going on. An older couple shields their eyes from the sun to see more clearly the woman screaming. As I reach the closest tent, I see their looks of concern. Flori's screams are approaching hysteria, and I am torn about what to do next. Looking back at her, I struggle to know how to end this. *Should I run and return to her?* A younger couple standing near the closest tent look from Flori to me, also trying to understand what is happening. The husband takes several steps toward me as if he wants to introduce himself, but there is no time for a conversation.

I look him in the eye, and yell, "Have you seen a boy? Our son is missing!" This question only requires a "Yes" or a "No."

But the man asks, "How old is he?"

The question feels like a blow to my chest. If they need to ask, Marius is not with them. Other approaching campers ask, "Where did you see him last?" and "What is his name?"

If Marius is not at the camp, then I do not want to take the time to answer. I turn and see Flori pointing to the ground near the small hole.

CHAPTER 5

Beside the road from Murighiol to Tulcea
August 6, 1991, about 3:00 p.m.
Flori

AT FIRST, ALL I CAN hear is the terrifying silence. Gone are the slight sounds of Marius's song, a stick being dragged across the grass, or a sixteen-month-old jumping off the concrete foundation ledge. Now that we have finished searching all the logical hiding nooks and crannies in which Marius could have playfully hidden, the search has taken on an entirely different urgency. Charlie's face and body movements convey his growing panic and it strikes a terrible fear inside me. I watch Charlie check the tall pipe again. It seems to be sealed, but I am not convinced. "What do you see there? Is Marius there?"

Charlie's confused expression tells me he does not see Marius. I suddenly need to go to the pipe, so I begin to run toward Charlie. The pressure in my chest increases. It feels like a thousand ants are climbing up my chest. They swarm and climb and tumble on top of each other to reach my heart and prevent another heartbeat. The pain becomes unbearable. Charlie, who seems to have suddenly abandoned all the other possible explanations, sprints toward the tents.

"Stop! Stop! No, no. My baby is here!" I shout to Charlie. I point to the area behind the sealed pipe. "You need to go there!" I am drawn to the grass behind the tall pipe like a magnet, and on my knees, I begin frantically to search the grassy area. I don't understand my obsession. *How do I know my baby boy is under this grass?* But I cannot stop calling out to Charlie, "My baby is here! Here is my baby!"

Charlie ignores my cries, which frustrates me enormously, but even I do not see any reason why I am so certain. Then suddenly, my hand hits the rough concrete around the small hole, and I stop. All that is there is a pipe that seems way too small. But I know. I hate it, but I know with an unexplainable certainty our son is somehow wedged down this hole. This dark hole is so terrifying no one would choose to believe it is true. But Marius is here, and I am not leaving. The ants rage in my chest, and I no longer feel my heartbeat or hear my own screams for help. But I do scream and keep screaming, "My boy is here!"

Charlie has made it across the field and is talking to several people by the tents. I scream loudly and don't know if Charlie hears me, but he turns back to look. I know he has seen the pipe and believes a toddler could not tumble into something so small. I think he has heard my screams because soon he is running across the field again. Several campers follow him. Others begin to spread out, calling Marius's name, and looking toward the road and the river's edge. I realize he has convinced people to help us!

Once he arrives, we say nothing to each other. I made a small gesture toward the pipe, "There, he is there." Charlie looks again at the small opening. A ray of light sparkles just off the center of the circle of dark water. Only two small pieces of grass float on the surface. As Charlie looks at me, I whimper, "My baby is there." In frustration, he looks me directly in my eyes and says, "It is too shallow!"

I repeat, "Marius is there. I know he is down there." I do not look at Charlie; I point to the pipe.

Once again, Charlie looks down and says, "What do you see? Nothing! There is nothing to see. It is impossible for Marius to have fallen down there! Stop screaming! You are distracting everyone from searching, and we need their help!"

But I continue to scream, "*My boy* is here!" And I will not move.

Charlie closes his eyes and shakes his head at me. But I will not move, and I shake my head back at him.

"Oh, Flori!" he groans, turns, and races back toward the tents. He grabs a broom handle resting against the tent support posts. He charges across the field for the fourth time. I know his determined look, the set of his jaw, and I understand he is coming to prove me wrong. I hope he is right.

As he approaches me, he raises the broom handle well above his head and vigorously thrusts it into the pipe. "It is too shallo—" But Charlie does not finish the word. For instead of having the broom handle hit the mud of a shallow pool of water with a solid thud, the broom keeps going down. The lack of any resistance catches Charlie off balance, and he stumbles. He recovers his balance and kneels down, letting the broomstick sink into the water as far as he can reach. He is shocked and suddenly overcome with doubt and then fear. His expression reflects the possibility I am right, and his thoughts and plans are scrambled. He has wanted to prove me wrong and move on to find our son who only has mischievously wandered away. I understand all of this because I don't want our sweet baby to be hidden in this silent, dark pipe.

Charlie examines the opening more closely. It does look a little different! Grass has grown around, obscuring the pipe's edges. "It is a few inches wider than I had expected," Charlie says as the color in his faces drains. I look, and it is maybe twelve to fourteen inches. It still looks too small, but now we know it is not shallow. He looks up at me and shakes his head.

"No."

I nod. I know he feels and shares the same despair. As he begins a much more earnest inspection of the pipe, I begin hysterically calling Marius's name. My hands go from my head to my broken heart. I want to escape, so I run a few steps, and then I turn back to be nearer my baby. "He is there. I know he is!" Without a plan, Charlie seems lost too. My words fade to a whisper. "He is there." My mother-insistence is unrelenting.

A small group of campers and other vacationers, who had been enlisted for an immediate search, return shaking their heads that they have seen no sign of our son. In the distance, I can still hear others calling Marius's name.

I tell him, "He is there. I know where he is, and he is down there."

An older man leans over to look into the pipe and begins shaking his head.

His weathered eyes close, and he makes little clicking sounds with his tongue. "Lady, I saw your baby playing, and it is impossible. The pipe is too small. He is too fat." He points to the pipe. "It is much too small."

"No, you are wrong. I know Marius is there!"

Murmuring begins within the small group. Someone says that I don't know what I am saying. The couple looks at me, and the husband gestures, "You are wrong. It cannot be."

Seeing the flash of anger in my eyes, Charlie jumps up between us. The man turns away, as do other onlookers who leave to search elsewhere. Some just avert their eyes, too traumatized to watch our despair. I hear Charlie explain that he understands the man's reasonable doubt. The hole looks too small, but he has experienced my intuition before. It is clear to me now—Charlie will defend me and not leave my side. I am taking a stand and not going anywhere. We are working together to save our son.

We have no answers, so we exchange several rapid questions. Might Marius have passed through the pipe to the lake or even the river? What should we do first? Charlie reaches up and rubs the back of his neck. He looks around, and we both see the crowd's sympathy, but they encourage one another to keep looking elsewhere. We don't even understand the situation, much less how to find our son.

Charlie drops to his knees again next to me, cutting them on the ragged concrete that surrounds the small pipe. He lowers the broom into the water, leaning down and extending his reach to his shoulder. The deeper he pushes the broomstick, the more a force pushes upward. This opposing pressure forces the broomstick to hit against the side of the pipe, and I watch as he struggles to keep it in the middle. Instinctively Charlie gets down on his stomach, extending his right arm and then even his shoulder into the hole.

I kneel next to him, and he mumbles loudly enough for me to hear, "It's hitting something that is not as solid as mud. It gives with the broom's pressure." He pushes harder, but it is more difficult to push down—the resistance has increased.

"You can do it." I pat his arm. Since we haven't seen Marius, it is confusing to explain what we are even trying to do. But it feels right that we are doing something! With this second effort, I can see the broom handle drop lower as the object continues to move. Charlie brings the broom handle up high enough for us to see the end. "There is no mud on the bottom of the stick," I whisper.

"What did I hit?" he asks. "What is in the pipe that the broom handle moves?" He sits up and wipes his eyes with his hands.

I wonder, *What are we to do now?*

Leaning over the pipe and positioning myself to allow as much sunlight as possible to shine into the pipe, I am the first to see him. Three feet below the top of the pipe, the awful truth is slowly floating to the surface. Marius's beautiful, soft curls, and then the very top of his head are now visible in the small, elliptical spot of light within the pipe.

"The baby! He is there! There on the surface!"

At first, the remaining crowd murmurs their disbelief, but Charlie immediately leans forward and sees him too. "Marius!" Those darling curls of baby hair mean there is no need to look anywhere else. The people call to those still searching, and all who hear run over. No one offers any opinions or suggestions. At the pipe, only silence screams our horror.

CHAPTER 6

Beside the road from Murighiol to Tulcea
August 6, 1991, about 3:09 p.m.
Charlie

OVERCOMING THE IMMEDIATE SHOCK AND disbelief, I kneel down extending my arm and shoulder into the hole. I can feel the pipe's ragged edge tear my neck and ear. My arm almost fills the pipe, so neither Flori nor I can see into it any longer. I was certain I would be able to reach our baby, but I cannot.

It may be the position or my failure to succeed, but I find breathing impossible. I sit up, and the air rushes out of my lungs. Everyone can hear my loud, primal moan, and they echo it as they share our frustration.

"I cannot reach him," I admit.

The defensive driving strategies I teach at work began to race through my mind at a blinding speed. Drivers need instantly to consider options when an accident seems probable. Here were the options I recognize immediately:

1. remove the concrete around the hole,
2. dig down,
3. break the pipe.

But all of these require tools and more time than this fight for life allows. We need an ax even to think about doing any of that quickly. I ask if anyone has an ax, but no one volunteers one. "Not even at the campsite? There are none?" I repeat in disbelief.

"No, no. We don't have one. Maybe a shovel." The older man shakes his head.

A woman leaves, calling to someone at the campsite. But no one can find the shovel or any other tool. I take a deep breath and rub my face in the reflection. More people arrive and press in toward where we kneel. Their disbelief our son has fallen into such a small hole annoys me. I do not even answer them. What is the use? We are beyond disbelief, and I do not have time to explain. Seeing my frustrations, other campers argue that we are the parents, and we have seen his hair and head. They insist it is true. I know everyone wants to help save the baby, but no one suggests a realistic rescue. We do not have tools, such as a pole with a hook. I understand we do not have time. We need to pull him up, and we need to use what we do have. I am the tallest, with the longest arm span. And I am Marius's father. I am not giving up my place at the pipe.

CHAPTER 7

Beside the road from Murighiol to Tulcea
August 6, 1991, about 3:11 p.m.
Flori

CHARLIE'S LOUD AND UNNERVING MOAN sends a chilling fear into my heart. I am certain I will explode into a million pieces if I do not touch my baby boy. His terror is my terror; his brokenness is my brokenness. I need to touch him the way I did when he was in his crib at night whimpering from a bad dream. My touch was enough to end his nightmares and comfort Marius. Touching him would be enough to make things better. Touching him, even if it is only with the stick, will be more to hold than what I have now in my empty hand.

I grab the stick at Charlie's knee, lean over the pipe, and lower it down along the side.

"God, let him live. I don't want him to die, but I prefer to be separated from him than to have him die. But let him live." I don't know the God I am praying to, and the words make no sense to me, but they are the words that form in my heart, and I utter them in sincere ignorance.

Then the broom handle touches something, and it moves downward. I can feel it sink. Withdrawing the broom handle a little, I can now see down inside the pipe again. The circle of sunlight still sparkles, but in the shadow, I see something different. Marius's little arm is above his head, gently wrapped around the broom handle. I blink to see if he is grasping it, but he is not. Although his face is still below the water, I can see his fingers and his little palm are slightly above the surface of the water.

"Charlie, look. Maybe you can reach him now! Look at his left arm. It is up!" With one quick look down the pipe, Charlie kneels down next to the pipe. He braces his left arm on the grass on the far side and above the opening, and he reaches into the hole with his right arm, again extending his shoulder. He has to pull his face awkwardly to the side. I hold my breath as Charlie stretches out to grab our son's life.

I whisper into his ear, "You can reach him."

"I got him. I can reach his hand." Charlie is overcome with relief. "I have four of his fingertips."

CHAPTER 8

Beside the road from Murighiol to Tulcea
August 6, 1991, about 3:11 p.m.
Charlie

I WAS SO HAPPY TO touch Marius's fingers. I was so proud to tell Flori. But the fingers do not grasp back. They are profoundly different from the fingers that traced my morning beard hours before. They are cold and stiff. But this is more than I had just a few minutes ago, and it has to be enough to get him up and into Flori's arms. Slowly, Flori lifts the broom handle out of the pipe to make more room.

The hushed crowd exchanges surprise and encouragement. But as soon as I begin to lift him up, the extreme difficulty of the task immediately is obvious. Marius's hand is wet and slimy from the stagnant water, and my hand soon becomes equally wet and slippery. As I begin to lift the baby out of the water, Marius's weight increases. I cannot bend my elbow. To raise him, I need to lift with my knees and a stiff arm. The pressure on my shoulder, the necessary awkward movement, and my cramping hand are suddenly immediate threats to getting him up.

I bite my lips and squeeze my fingers against Marius's as much as possible. Slowly our fingers began to lose traction. Slowing my lift seems only to make it worse. I begin to put more pressure on my knees and left arm, trying to pull up faster.

"I am losing him," I confess to Flori. In anguished slow-motion, Marius's fingers slip more. I can feel them sliding, and at the same time I feel Flori patting my shoulder and calmly saying, "No, you have him."

But her willing it to be so does not change the fact that I feel his weight increasing as I pull him out of the water, and our fingers begin slipping again.

"I am losing him," I groan.

"No, bring me my baby," Flori cries out.

I squeeze his fingers, shut my eyes, and clench my teeth. But my will cannot stop the slow slipping from my grasp. First one baby finger, and then another slides away. I want to believe this rescue will work until his last small finger slips between my numb fingers, and I understand I am holding onto nothing.

"I lost him."

Probably only Flori and I, with our ears at the pipe, hear the soft sound of our son dropping down, sinking, and disappearing below the water's surface. But I will never forget it.

It is all too much. It crushes me, and I rock back on my knees. I cover my face with my hands. The rank odor of the algae almost causes me to vomit. I vigorously wipe my palms on my pants and shirt, and I swallow the bitter taste and thought that Marius is now under such stink.

Collectively, the small crowd gasps as though they have been holding their breaths. Mothers pick up their young children, hold them tightly, and walk away. This is too much to share.

A younger man drops to his knees and says, "Try again. You can do it this time." Others repeat, "Don't give up."

I use their encouragement to look into the pipe again. There is no sign of the top of Marius's head or the curl of his hair. Only the ripples on the water's surface dance in the elliptical light.

"Where did the baby go?" Flori moves to the side of the pipe to try to let more light into the hole.

No one answers. What can I say to my wife, Marius's devoted mother? I am overwhelmed with a new and powerful despair. There is no one to help me. I am truly alone and powerless. And for the first time I know I need help from someone greater than myself. I am completely lost.

CHAPTER 9

Beside the road from Murighiol to Tulcea
August 6, 1991, about 3:12 p.m.
Flori

"Do you see him?" I feel my heart rip in two, as I just stare down into the black hole.

I have a tight grip on Charlie's arm. Neither of us has any awareness of anything happening outside of that small opening. It takes concentration even to remember to breathe. Maybe we don't. A sudden flicker of light bounces inside and onto the water's surface. I feel Charlie tighten his grip on my hand.

"There, I see him. He is coming back up," I whisper.

"Yes, yes, his hair, I see him too." Charlie is suddenly confident with a surge of new strength. Having nothing to grasp but this renewed hope, I gently push the wooden broom handle down again along the side of the pipe.

More calmly than I feel, I say, "And his left arm is up again. It is around the stick. I will hold the broomstick still to guide you." I am no longer frantic. I see our baby's head again. Determination replaces panic. Hope floods in. I can feel Charlie moving into action. I am amazed we will have a second chance. What can we do differently?

I tell him, "I will give you directions. Follow the directions and grab him and bring him out." If I make it sound simple, maybe it will be simple.

Charlie rips off his shirt, declaring, "I will get him this time. I can reach him, but I need two hands."

Quickly, Charlie tries to see if he can get two arms down the hole. If he can, then he will rely on others to pull him and the baby up. Putting two arms into the pipe removes the balance his left arm had provided, so he stretches out on his stomach. Immediately, it is clear he will not successfully reach down with both arms. The wedge shape formed by his shoulders will limit his ability to extend his shoulders down into the pipe. Charlie doesn't hesitate. He remains on his stomach, and just his right arm reaches down as he had done before. He follows my directions to use the stick as a guide for his blind attempt. When he reaches Marius's fingers, I lift the broom handle out to make room. My plan works, and he tells me he is grasping the small fingers again.

"I have more of them this time, maybe most of all of them." Charlie's voice quietly fills with conviction. I feel my own hope grow.

And then I wrap my arms around his middle and begin to help him lift Marius. The weight of our child's wet body increases again as we lift him out of the water, and Charlie's moan warns me he fears he will drop our son again.

"Stop. Marius's fingers are sliding. He is too heavy. I need to lower him back into the water without losing my grip. I will keep his face above the surface."

I let Charlie roll closer to the pipe, and I listen for the awful sound of the baby dropping back below the surface. My husband keeps hold of what little of the baby's fingers are still in his grasp. It seems like a controlled defeat. Charlie rolls over onto one side and looks up at me.

The concrete cuts into Charlie's neck. I ignore the bleeding wounds just as Charlie does. And suddenly, I see a new path.

"I will reach in with you and help grab him." I didn't need to say more, as we both instantly know the plan without explanation. While still grasping the baby's fingers, Charlie turns even more onto his side, and I lie alongside and in front of him. I can lower my right arm down next to his. As I extend my arm, Charlie pulls up. The weight increases again, the fingers slipping from the water and algae just as before. But this time, as Charlie pulls up just a bit more, I can rotate my wrist, and with my dry hand grab below the baby's wrist.

"Okay?" Charlie whispers into my ear.

I nod.

"Okay!" Charlie hardly has time to say the word when with complete synchronization he lets go, and I hold onto and then pull Marius up a few inches. Charlie immediately grabs even lower on Marius's arm, almost to the elbow. I do not let go, but we are stuck as neither of us can bend our elbows. Once I feel the strength and speed of Charlie's lift, I let go and roll to the side. In a second, Charlie has Marius up and on the grass between us!

For a second, I am confused. This is not our child. The familiar clothes are the only convincing evidence that we have indeed succeeded and freed our trapped son. Disbelief fills my heart. It is impossible to recognize Marius. His face, arms, hands, and legs are dark blue, perhaps black. His body is swollen, so swollen the clothes look sizes too small. And his arms and legs bulge at the edges of the sleeves and shorts. His face is two or three times the size it should be. His nose so swollen that his nostrils flare, reaching the edges of his engorged cheeks. His mouth is open in a circle, like the center of a donut. His lips are so big they almost cover the nearby parts of the nostrils and his chin. His eyes are squeezed tightly closed. Where is our curious, happy, little boy? The absolute stillness of the baby's body completes the horrific scene. We look at each other and wonder, "What should we do next?" Neither Charlie nor I know.

We just stare down at Marius. The crowd steps back, understanding at that moment how victory can quickly change to tragedy.

CHAPTER 10

Beside the road from Murighiol to Tulcea
August 6, 1991, about 3:15 p.m.

THE CROWD BEGAN TO REACT with comments that expressed their obvious grief. "Mother of God, have mercy."

"Oh no."

Families cried out and hugged each other, and they mourned as though one of their own had died.

"How long was he down there?" a new onlooker asked a man standing alone.

The man just shook his head, gesturing it had been too long. "At least eight minutes. His parents fought so hard just to rescue," he choked up. Bringing his fingers over his eyes, he continued, "Their dead son." Overcome again, the man walked away sobbing.

Flori looked down. She knew how to check for a heartbeat from attending nursing school for two years. She reached to take a pulse from the wrist, but she could feel none. The coldness of Marius's skin caused her to pull her fingers back. She lowered her ear to his chest—silence. There were neither breathing sounds nor movement. Charlie was also assessing for life. He found none.

Flori suddenly knew she needed to get the water out of the lungs. She had been taught a spinning technique for children who had drowned. Although she had seen it demonstrated, she had only practiced with a medical doll. What else was there to do? She grabbed Marius's feet, stood up, and started to turn around and around. The spinning created a powerful centrifugal force causing the baby's body to fly outward. His arms flung wildly beyond his head.

"She is hysterical! Crazy!" a man in a red shirt whispered to his daughter as he walked away.

Charlie too wondered what she was doing. "Flori, don't," he tried whispering to her.

Without slowing down, Flori shouted, "I know what to do. Let me do it. I have to get the water from his lungs. Let me do what I know to do!" Her hands were slippery, and she had to grasp Marius's legs with all her strength. Even then she could feel them slipping until she was holding tightly only to the baby's ankles.

A woman in the crowd cried, "No! Stop! He's been through enough."

Charlie looked at the woman and Flori's increasingly fast spinning. She was turning so fast that she was leaning back against the baby's weight, and the uneven ground caused her to wobble. Marius's arms were flying outward, disturbingly flopping and knocking into each other.

Flori had more medical training than Charlie. He had seen her quickly give first aid to others with admirable competence. He trusted her, and he needed to let her do what she wanted. Everyone else thought Marius was dead. Only Flori seemed to have hope. Charlie wanted this hope too, and he had no better plan. Neither did the crowd, which had begun to mourn. So Charlie decided to trust Flori.

"Stop her! She has gone mad," another man said as the whirling continued.

A newcomer who had joined the crowd and said, "No, this is what she needs to do. My uncle does this with newborn lambs if they are born and do not breathe. It might help pull the water out of his lungs."

Around and around Flori and her son rotated—eight, nine, ten times. Flori began to feel dizzy, and her hands were still wet and unusually slippery from the algae. She began to collapse, and falling into Charlie she cried, "Help me! Help me put him down."

Charlie put his arms around first her, and then the baby. A man and a woman in the crowd joined them, and together they put the baby down softly onto the grass.

No water had appeared to run out from his lungs. Marius had not moved, and his appearance had not changed—he was still completely limp. Flori began to give chest compressions, which she would alternate with mouth-to-mouth resuscitation. The chest compressions continued for a minute or two, and then the individuals in the crowd began to look to Charlie to intervene.

The overwhelming sadness that other parents were witnessing was heart-wrenching.

A woman cried, "How could this have happened?"

Flori heard her. A wave of guilt surged through her body. It was the pain of her chest and heart being torn apart. She beat back the pain by applying the compressions. If she stopped, it meant death not only for her son, but also for herself.

The woman's husband said, "Why do that? You're breaking his bones. Now? Lady, he's dead already."

Charlie saw the look in Flori's eyes. The helplessness and the pain transformed into rage. Her eyes flashed, and her body tensed like a tiger's. Charlie thought Flori would pounce if it didn't mean she would have to stop her desperate efforts. Charlie stepped in between his wife and the couple. Their intervention was well-intended, but it was not welcome. Later he would wonder if he had moved to protect them or Flori, but it hadn't mattered. It was clear Flori had not given up.

What was painfully obvious to everyone else standing above the small, lifeless baby lying on the grass was not possible for her to believe. She only knew her son needed help, and no one was offering any.

Suddenly frothy foam began to gush from the baby's mouth and nose. She looked for his struggle to breathe, but he remained still. She turned his head for the water to run out. The soft bubbles stopped. Seeing the bubbles form near Marius's mouth, Charlie dropped down and pressed his ear against the baby's chest. He expected to hear something. All he heard was absolute silence. There was no sound of a struggle to breathe.

"Our son needs a doctor!" Maybe everyone in the small group watching this tragedy was on vacation. They had little knowledge of the area, or perhaps, they were too traumatized to answer. Certainly, some believed not even a doctor could help this poor, little boy. But no one offered any help or suggestions. The Madas were in a remote place, and they felt absolutely alone. There was no one else to call on for help. Charlie and Flori exchanged a look that said it all.

"We're going to have to find a doctor."

"Let's go!" Charlie was relieved to have a mission. They would get their baby to a doctor as fast as possible. He scooped up Marius, and they raced toward the car. He knew driving toward Tulcea was the best chance to get medical help.

CHAPTER 11

Stopping in Mahmudia, on road from Murighiol to Tulcea
August 6, 1991, about 3:22 p.m.
Flori

CHARLIE GETS TO THE CAR first, and I grab his keys from his belt, and open the passenger door to jump in. Charlie puts Marius on my lap. He remains limp, cold, blue-black, and swollen beyond recognition. His legs flop off my lap, and I am shocked as his little arms dangle, freely without purpose. So I tuck his legs up on my lap and draw his arms into my embrace. It is like the first week we had him, bundled up in swaddling blankets. I couldn't take my eyes off of our new son for days, but today I cannot look at his face. I bring him up against my chest and continue modified chest compressions by drawing him close and tight against my body, and then releasing. I just need to hug him and warm him with the heat of my own body.

I cannot understand what has suddenly happened. I cannot think of these last moments and hold myself together. I try to think of Marius charming the waiter at the restaurant just hours ago. I think of his laughter and sparkling eyes, but it only works for seconds. It isn't then; it is now, and I must give a puff of breath into his cold mouth. This is all I can do now. I tell myself, "It is enough. Our son will live."

Charlie pulls out of the grassy shoulder and turns right, toward Tulcea. The two-lane road again wanders through the wilderness. The flat, treeless marsh and grassland increase my feelings of being small, needy, and alone. Neither of us says very much. The wind across the open window occasionally makes a frightful moan. But the sad sound doesn't seem out of place or disturbing, because it precisely expresses the darkness that haunts us in our unspoken fears.

Rounded, treeless mountains seem to loom a constant distance away. They fill the horizon ahead, and they stand there in a violet haze, unaware of our desperate flight to reach the help that lies beyond them. Charlie accelerates on the straight stretches and carefully downshifts into sharp turns to the right, and then the left. We pass wooden horse carts. They are driven by farmers who have lived their entire lives here, unaware of hidden pipes and other man-made dangers.

Soon, Charlie slows to pass safely through the village of Mahmudia. Houses stand close to the road's curb. A lone tree, twisted and gnarled by the wind, clings to a small patch of dirt. A Red Cross sign, which is nailed on the trunk, points to a hospital.

"Do you see it? Turn right, Charlie!"

Charlie turns right. I look over and think, "He trusts me. He stood up to those people who were so ready to believe the worst. They saw the worst before they had even tried to save Marius. We are going to do this." Although I still cannot look into a face that contradicts my hope, I continue to press the baby against my chest, closing my eyes to blow firmly into his mouth several times a minute.

My husband's trust and respect increase my own hope. Marius will be well again. That idea grows between us.

The small town of Mahmudia is a confusing maze of streets. "Ask him!" I say, pointing to a businessman carrying a newspaper under his arm.

Charlie rolls down the window and urgency calls, "Where's the hospital? I need a doctor for my son!"

The man looked confused, and he comes over to Charlie's window. Once he sees me holding the blanket wrapped around a small child, he answers, "Turn left and then look for the Red Cross on the lower floor of the third building."

"This cannot be right," Charlie shouts. "It is only an apartment. We are in a residential area. Where is the hospital?"

"There is a sign above the basement door."

The Red Cross on the side of the building looks worn, but the office door is visible. Breathlessly we burst inside. "We need help! Our baby needs help!" I shout again to a young woman wearing a white lab coat and nurse's cap. "We need help now. Where is the doctor?"

"There is no doctor. It is only me. There is no one else here but me."

The room is only about fifteen by twelve feet, with a single stretcher on the right wall, a desk, and one large, white cabinet with glass doors filled with boxes of medicine.

"Where is the hospital?" Charlie demands.

The nurse says, "This is the emergency first aid service. It is not a hospital. I only have a stethoscope," which she touches as she shrugs her shoulders. "I have nothing more."

"Well, we need an oxygen machine. He was under water, and we need to give him oxygen." I begin to unwrap our son from the blanket. Seeing Marius's distorted and swollen face and the dark blue coloring, the nurse gasps and cries out hysterically.

"I have nothing to help you. I only have this." She touches the stethoscope draped from her neck again. She brings the palm of her hand up to her forehead and begins to rub it back and forth, raising her bangs into a tangled mess. As she approaches the stretcher on which we have placed Marius, she weeps loudly, "What can I do to help? What could even a doctor do for him?"

"No!" I put my hand up. I am not going to trust Marius to this woman. If I can remain focused and calm enough to do all that has been required, I am not going to let someone who is repulsed by the way my precious son looks now touch him. But the whole truth is that I am shocked by the sight of him too. Her hysteria threatens that I too will lose control. I refuse to see our son through her eyes, so I stand between her and Marius and demand, "I need rubbing alcohol!"

"I told you, I have nothing." The nurse's eyes dart around the room. Charlie pointed to the medicine cabinet that is filled with boxes.

"No. No! They are all empty. They are for show." She goes over and opens the glass doors. Then she begins throwing them down onto the floor. The impact of the empty boxes on the floor is hardly heard above her cries.

I ignore her dramatics. "I need to rub him with rubbing alcohol. I need to increase his circulation."

The nurse stops crying and walks timidly closer to the stretcher. She moves the stethoscope around and listens to Marius's chest. Shaking her head back and forth, she simply says, "No. I cannot hear anything."

I do not acknowledge her. "Charlie, go out and ask the neighbors for rubbing alcohol. Or ask for vinegar." He leaves immediately, and just as quickly, he returns carrying a half-filled but large bottle.

I form a silent truce with the young nurse. She follows my lead in cutting the clothing off. It is extremely difficult to get one blade of the scissors under his shirt to cut it off. The appearance of more black/blue skin is shocking. His body seems even more swollen and still. I pretend I do not see the stillness, and I take the bottle and begin to splash vinegar over Marius's chest and arms, filling the room with the strong, pungent smell. We rub vigorously, ignoring the strong effect the vinegar has on our eyes. Charlie and the nurse finish cutting the baby's shorts off, while I begin rubbing the skin on his legs. The skin began to fade from black/blue toward dark gray, and then even lighter gray. The nurse uses the stethoscope to listen again. She takes her time. She finishes, but she does not look up into our eyes. She just shakes her head and collapses once again into tears and choking cries.

I am impatient with her, "Stop it. I will do it myself. You are not helping. Go! Call for help. Call for an ambulance."

"It is over thirty minutes away," the nurse cries. But she obediently picks up the phone and dials.

The conversation is short, "Hur-rrr-ry the baby was submerged. He is dark blue. No, bluuue to gray. There is no heartbeat. He is not breathing." She then turns away toward the wall and whispers into the phone. When she hangs up, she does not return to my side. She sinks down into the desk chair and puts her hands to her face and continues to cry softly.

Without saying goodbye, we leave.

CHAPTER 12

On the road from Mahmudia to Tulcea
August 6, 1991, est. 3:40 p.m.
Charlie

ONCE WE ARE OUT OF town and on the open road, I begin to recall what I said to the young nurse. "Tell the ambulance we will drive toward the hospital on the same road. We will also have the headlights on. They should look for that, and when we see them, we will honk the horn and pull over on the side of the road to transfer Marius." But I cannot hear if she repeats the instructions. I may need to drive all the way to the hospital.

I don't ask if we had wasted valuable time getting to a real hospital by following the signs to an empty Red Cross station. It had seemed like such a relief when we first saw the international red and white cross, but nothing has been accomplished.

I quickly glance over at my wife. I see in her hope. Flori never hesitated—she knew what to do. Without all of her quick thinking, I could not have raised Marius from the pipe. She has a confident hope that he will live. Flori doesn't smile but says softly, "I feel better away from the pipe, away from those people, away from that silly nurse. You did good getting him out of the pipe." She looks at me and nods.

I feel good that she has said that, but I wonder if our boy is dead. There is no movement, no giggling, no chattering, and no laughter. I have seen nothing that looks like our active, adorable son. This doesn't even look like Marius sleeping.

I carefully negotiate the unfamiliar town streets, weaving in and around the traffic, and then make the sharp turn onto the main road toward the city. I have my lights on and use the horn to indicate there is an emergency. Most of the drivers followed the law and pulled up onto the sidewalk or the road's narrow shoulder, allowing us to pass. I am driving faster and riskier than my wife has ever seen, but I am confident. And she doesn't show any sign of disapproval. This road is fairly empty of traffic, and I press down on the accelerator. The sound of tires on uneven pavement pounds out our progress. Neither of us speaks, as we each also try to navigate our desperate fears.

I hope an ambulance will meet us halfway, but I know that if I hadn't stopped and driven there directly, we would have reached the Tulcea Hospital sooner. The hope I had before the First Aid Station is harder to nurture or share. Next to me, Flori continues the unorthodox chest compressions by pulling our baby in toward her body. The silence is intolerable.

Flori whispers, "Why did I tell him to be quieter so often?"

"No, no Flori. Don't," I say. But I am thinking the same thing. I want my son to make noise—annoying noises or silly songs or unrelenting clapping sounds. I want a second chance to accept the noise and extra work of being a father. But Marius is silent and still.

CHAPTER 13

Halfway from Mahmudia to Tulcea
August 6, 1991, est. 3:50 p.m.
Flori

I AM COLD AND SHIVERING. My body needs clear cognitive commands to do simple things. I intentionally repeated to myself, "Release; blow firmly into his lips." But I also hear my heart whisper, "Don't look too closely at your baby's cold, blue lips."

I silently tell Marius, "Show me a sign. Move! Cry! Squirm?" I promise this tiny still body, now lost in vinegar-soaked blankets, "I will not worry about those types of things again when you are better."

The trip is expected to take a total of about thirty minutes, but with light traffic and Charlie's driving skill and his disregard for the speed limits, I spot the approaching white and red ambulance within ten minutes. The ambulance driver flashes his lights in response to Charlie's light signaling and horn. They each pull over onto the grassy shoulder. I struggle to get out of the car carrying Marius, and race across the empty road. The back doors open, and I hand the baby up into the ambulance. Someone helps me up the high back step into the back of the EMV.

I say, "He needs oxygen."

The doors slam shut, and I look back through the small window for my husband. He is also looking across the street for me. Our eyes meet, but we don't smile. The ambulance makes a full U-turn and pulls out in front of Charlie. The transfer doesn't take more than a minute.

Once inside the back of the ambulance, I realize I have handed my son to a female doctor in a white coat. I am left weak and collapse onto the bench across from the cot where Marius lies. I am relieved to hand over the responsibility and trust to someone with more skill and experience. The doctor does not introduce herself, nor did she begin any care. She looks at the baby, his gray to blue color and his motionless chest. She wrote something in the chart, and then she sits and does nothing.

I repeat, "He needs oxygen!"

"I am in control now. I know what has to be done," the doctor states without looking at me.

I am alarmed. I take a deep breath, look at the woman, and understand the doctor is expecting me to respect her authority. I remember the young nurse talking on the phone with her back to us, and I wonder what she has said about Marius, or even Charlie and me.

I attempt to relax and allow the doctor to begin to assess Marius. However, she doesn't place her stethoscope near his chest. She doesn't search for a pulse at his small wrist or neck. She just sits there. I am leaning against the ambulance wall, and I lean forward and try to look into the doctor's eyes. Was the woman thinking or having a spell that keeps her from taking care of Marius? The woman just looks forward toward the driver and remains silent.

I began rubbing my son's skin again, taking his little legs in my hands and rubbing up and down from his toes to just above his knees. I whisper again, "He needs oxygen. He was submerged."

But instead of leaning over and helping me, the doctor leans over and waves her index finger back and forth. "No, no, no. I am in charge here. I know what needs to be done."

I give her a serious stare, keep my mouth closed and think, *In charge of what? Of doing nothing? Of not helping a child who desperately needs her help?* I sit back in shock and disbelief. No oxygen, no checking for a heartbeat? What is this woman in charge of doing? I begin to wonder if the woman in the white coat is a doctor or just someone who rides in the ambulance.

Just as the helplessness and overwhelming confusion settles into my heart, Marius goes into a violent convulsion. The movement is so strong and unexpected that both of us jump and utter our surprise. His body arches from head to toe in a rigid, shaking movement. The doctor looks at me, and I see her fear and disbelief. She jumps back and away from him.

"Oxygen!" I repeated firmly.

The doctor reaches across the cot and listens to the baby's heart. She listens and then removes the earbuds from her ears and shakes her head to say—nothing.

When the driver of the ambulance hears the doctor's surprised gasp, he slows down. A quick look over his shoulder confirms something dramatic has occurred, and he begins to pull off the road.

"No! No! Don't stop! We need to get to the hospital," I say. I don't want this doctor in charge of our baby's care for even one moment longer than necessary. I begin chest compressions without permission.

The doctor steps forward and moves into the passenger's seat to reassure the driver. "To the hospital, fast." Then she reaches over and picks up the microphone. Someone must have picked up and answered at the hospital. "This is serious! Be ready!"

I continue the chest compressions and occasionally rub Marius's legs. His little body relaxes enough for me to push his chest gently down on the cot by leaning all my weight on him. I expect the doctor to return and administer oxygen or CPR—but she does not. I search Marius's face for an encouraging sign, a movement, a small breath, a twitch. How could a convulsion be encouraging? I hoped it would quick-start his breathing, his life. But there is no sign it has accomplished anything good.

After the driver is told not to pull over, he drives faster. The closer we get to the hospital, the faster he drives. Charlie has been able to keep up, but increased city traffic makes it very difficult. I look out the rear window, but I lose sight of our car several times. Somehow, he manages to reach the hospital's doors at the same time we do. I shake my head, "No change." Then I mouth the words for only him to understand. "No oxygen! Nothing."

CHAPTER 14

~~~~~~~~~~~~~~~~~~~~~~~~

Tulcea County Hospital, Romania
August 6, 1991, 4:05 p.m.

CHARLIE AND FLORI BOTH EXPECTED to enter the doors and have a team of doctors and nurses waiting to begin emergency care. But there was no one waiting. They had called ahead for preparation, specifically oxygen. Charlie saw nothing that reassured him they were even at a hospital. The lobby was empty except for a nurse sitting behind the admission desk.

Without looking up, the nurse asked, "Is this the child?" She continued to read and make notations on various forms.

The woman from the ambulance answers, "Yes. Where are the doctors?"

"They are not here. First, we need to complete the paperwork for admission, Doctor. Then we will call them."

For the first time, Flori and Charlie had confirmation the woman who had not offered any emergency care was really a medical doctor. Charlie's frustration raged. They had tried everything. They had done everything. They needed immediate help. Their child deserved medical help. Charlie kicked the closest chair with a force that surprised even him. The chair went flying across the room. The sound of the metal legs exploded and echoed in the empty waiting room. The nurse jumped up.

Charlie glared at her, "What are we going to do now?"

The ambulance doctor didn't flinch at the sound of the chair. With more confidence and determination than Charlie expected, she said, "We will go to the doctors in charge."

She went right to the elevator and pushed the button to go up. The nurse at the desk called to them, "At four o'clock. They are on the second floor, in the advanced and Special Care Ward."

The ambulance doctor stepped into the elevator and pushed the button marked "2." She showed no emotion but simply stated, "The second floor is the women's intensive and urgent care unit. A team of doctors will be checking on them at the hour."

The elevator rang two short tones, and the door opened and Charlie and Flori, who was still clutching her lifeless son in a blanket, followed the doctor into a small lobby. Two wooden doors directly across from the elevators were closed, but the doctor opened them and walked right down the center aisle between two rows—about twelve beds on each side. The metal beds each had a chart hanging at the foot, and various patients curled up and sleeping.

There were no visitors during the late afternoon rounds that were obviously in progress. Four doctors were in the middle of the room, looking at a chart and talking in quiet voices. They looked up at the approaching intrusion. One woman in a white coat and with a stethoscope around her neck walked toward them. They met at the bed of a young woman who, upon seeing the little blue arm dangling from the edge of the blanket and the faces of two anguished parents, got up and offered her bed.

Flori placed Marius on the bed, and the tallest doctor quickly leaned over and put the stethoscope to his chest. She checked for a pulse and breath, and then she reached into her pocket for a pen and ran it across the bottom of his foot. Marius did not react. She then touched the baby's skin—gray, dull, and cold. She lifted his little eye-lid and blew into his eye. No movement or reaction. Another doctor again tested the bottom of the baby's foot.

Flori could hear the other two doctors talking behind her. "Why did they bring the child here? There is nothing we can do." The doctor from the ambulance walked over and talked to one of the doctors near the door and then left. Flori's anger flared again. She did not respond; she kept silent. What she wanted to scream to everyone in the room was, "Stop asking me questions! Just do what you should be doing to help my son live!" Flori realized her anger wasn't likely to influence Marius's care at this point. She took a deep breath and looked intently at the doctor who had so professionally examined Marius.

The tall doctor asked gently, "Why did you bring the child here? We cannot do anything for him."

"He was black when we got him out of the pipe. We rubbed him with vinegar and did CPR, and now he is whitish. Please check him again. He has improved."

The doctors looked at Flori and then down at the baby. They didn't begin treatment, so Flori continued softly but firmly, "He was not given oxygen at the first aid station or in the ambulance. He needs oxygen to breathe. Please, we have worked so hard to get him here. Please give him oxygen."

Charlie looked at their son. He was so small lying on the bed. He was cold and slightly stiff. Charlie suspected what everyone but Flori believed. They did not see any life in Marius. Only Flori saw life. So Charlie followed Flori's lead, because the alternative was horrific. He was not about to go into such darkness alone. He chose to believe what his wife believed. He needed to stay close to her with his heart and not let his head listen to anything else.

The tall doctor listened carefully to Flori and then stepped closer. Putting her hand on Flori's arm, she gently asked, "Who are you?"

"We are the parents."

"Do you have other children?"

"No, he is our only child. After eight years waiting, there is only him. He is the only one. We cannot have any other children." They explained they had adopted Marius as a newborn.

Charlie added, "We brought him here for you to help him, to help us. Where else was there to go?"

"Please give him oxygen," Flori repeated her plea.

"Go outside and wait." Shaking her head, she said again, "You will need to wait outside."

Flori and Charlie just looked at her and then to the other doctors. That was an impossible request.

"Oxygen, he needs …" Flori reached out to touch the tall doctor's arm.

"Look at yourselves. You are bleeding. You are dirty. We cannot have you in here like this. We have patients recovering from surgery. Think of their families."

Flori looked at Charlie. She was shocked at what she saw. On his forehead, blotches and lines of dried, brown blood had drawn a map of his frustration and desperation. His neck and ears were covered with scratches and deep, ragged cuts from the pipe's edges. He was not wearing a shirt; neither of them had shoes. His shorts were discolored with the slimy pipe water mixed with grass and mud.

"Oh, Charlie. You are hurt." She reached out to his forehead and then his arms. But he pulled away.

"No, no. I am fine."

Flori didn't look any better. Her shirt was equally mixed with mud, grass, and dirty, stagnant water. But now she suddenly registered the odor of the baby's urine had mixed with the stench created by a struggle with fear and death.

Flori's weight shifted from one foot to the other. She looked away from the doctor and asked, "Why is there no oxygen? We rushed here, so you could give him oxygen to breathe." Flori did not make a move to leave.

The tall doctor walked to the head of the bed. She reached around to a small tank labeled "Oxygen" and pulled up a mask. Then she slowly placed an oxygen mask on Marius's face and adjusted the straps to tighten it. Looking up at Flori and Charlie, she gave them a small smile, one of kindness but not of hope. She gave the valve a short turn to the right. "There, I have done that." She did not look at the toddler's face.

Slowly, choosing her words deliberately, she continued, "Wash, change, and I will let you come back and stay with your baby." She came over to the couple and this time patted Charlie's arm. Firmly she led them down the long aisle toward the door. She carefully repeated, "You must wash, and then you can return."

Flori felt her hope drain from her chest. This was not the help she expected. She had little concern about dried blood and cuts and bruises that were no threat to their health. She was being asked to consider other patients' families. These patients were not in life-threatening conditions. How could there be such indifference and little effort to address her son's breathless body? He was just a little boy. He was full of adorable smiles and drooling kisses. They were not even looking at him. How could this be the care she and Charlie had so desperately desired since they pulled Marius from the pipe? Where else could they go?

Flori looked around, appealing to someone to offer much more than this. But there was no one. No one was looking on with sympathetic eyes. They had no advocate, no savior here. The nurse near the door took their arms and pushed them through the white, double doors. Charlie turned to ask a question, but the frosted glass prevented even a backward glance.

Flori and Charlie were standing in the elevator hallway as the second-floor ward's doors were firmly closed. And there they stood alone when the first tidal wave of grief crashed over and through them. They fell into each other's silent, violent sobs. In this desperate embrace, Flori's fingers dug into Charlie's arms, but the pain didn't match that of his shattered heart. Then the second wave hit Flori. This was the wave of indescribable guilt. Words could not come, but her brain registered the torrent of self-accusation. "How did I not watch him? I am not worthy to be a mother. I am responsible for him."

Over her silent screams, she felt her rock, her Charlie, shaking. It was too much. And together they broke down and slid down the wall to the floor. Loud, organic cries came from some deep, previously unknown depth. They could not breathe in this state of agony, and so they drained their last sob in gasping breaths. At that moment, only being with Marius was essential. Breathing seemed impossible if they could not see Marius.

CHAPTER 15

Tulcea County Hospital, Tulcea, Romania
August 6, 1991, 4:30 p.m.
Charlie

WITHIN MINUTES, AGAINST ALL MY emotions and desires, the storm is calmed. I find strength in my legs and stand up away from the wall. I reach out and hold the back of Flori's head and pull her close, kissing her forehead. I feel strength flow into her, and suddenly an unexplainable clarity of commitment replaces our tears. We need to focus on what we need to do to return to Marius's bedside. Our son is still here. He has an oxygen mask. He has not been declared dead by the doctors. We need to wash and change. Living has chosen us.

Flori looks at me and says, "Okay, you are a mess." Her eyes are red and tired, but also caring and soft. There is no insult, but neither of us smiles.

"And so are you," I say.

"Yes."

"And we smell too."

"Yes, we do. But you more than me."

Charlie managed a small smile. "Yes, I do. It is true."

"Let me see. Oh, you are cut around your armpit from the pipe. Some of them are deep. We need to clean them."

"I don't want to go to any doctor about this. They will take too much time. Call your aunt. She lives close to here. She can bring clean clothes." I point to a nearby office with a phone on the desk.

Unexpectedly, the doors of the recovery room open and startle us. The tall doctor walks out and scans the room before spotting us. I realize our cries have probably been heard through the doors. The nurses have heard our anguish. When we had suddenly stopped, a nurse was alarmed enough to call the doctor.

This tall doctor is bold. She has authority and is comfortable wearing it. I like her, and I look for her nametag: Doctor Mariana. I know immediately I can trust her.

She looks me in the eye, but she does not smile.

"Doctor Mariana," I address her with the confidence of my business experience.

"Yes."

"I'm Charlie Mada, and this is my wife and Marius's mother, Flori. We appreciate your care and concern for our son." My voice falters, and I must take a deep breath.

"Marius." My wife shifts her weight and puts her arm around my waist. She repeats, "Marius."

The doctor is professional and personable. She motions to see if we want to sit down. "Yes, Marius, Marius. Well, we are going to take care of both of you."

"You are going to take care of Marius." I can tell that Flori likes this doctor. She also understands this is the first time the doctor has said her son's name.

"Please, Doctor, concentrate only on Marius's care, not ours."

In Romania, there is no charge for medical services. It is considered the right of all citizens to have such care. However, because I have the means, I am expected to give a tip to receive extra attention. The money reassures me the medical staff knows our name, ability, and influence. And it is understood the staff will do more than the State requires. Although the practice is not legal, it is customary. I am prepared to offer a generous tip, so I pull out paper bills folded to display the large amount of money I am offering. It is ten times the normal amount they would expect, but I want our son to have every possible advantage of the best professional care.

"Thank you. We appreciate the care you will provide to *our son*." I purposely stress "our son." I like the way it sounds, and I also want to be clear that it isn't about caring for our comfort but Marius's health.

Doctor Mariana looks at the bills. Her eyes widen. She takes a step back and lifts both hands, palms open and above her shoulders. "No, no, Mr. Mada. I cannot take your money. Nothing has changed. He is not breathing, nor is there a heartbeat. I've done everything I can do. What can be done has been done. The situation has not changed. We will watch and see. Only God can make a miracle. I can do nothing more."

She is very polite and very firm. Respectfully, she does not wait for questions or conversation before disappearing behind the doors again.

I am shocked, and we look at each other. Neither of us has ever even heard of anyone being offered a tip and not accepting it. I am left with nothing more to do. *How could Doctor Mariana not accept this money?* I stuff it back into my pocket. *Does she want more money for such a serious case? Or is she afraid accepting the money would cause us to have expectations she might not meet?* Either way, I am not sure what to do next other than clean myself up and return to Marius's bedside.

CHAPTER 16

Tulcea County Hospital, Tulcea, Romania
August 6, 1991, 4:45 p.m.
Flori

I LIKE THIS LADY DOCTOR, but I am upset that Marius has become a "situation." The pressure in my chest returns, pressing against my throat. I have to get quickly washed and clean enough to be readmitted to the surgical floor and observe what medical care and treatment might be in progress. Charlie and I look at each other, and without a word, head for the office door again. We need to get to the phone to call my Aunt Cristina. My aunt and cousin are home and are more than willing to bring clean clothes to the hospital. As we leave the office, Dr. Mariana walks around the corner looking for us.

"Our clean clothes will be here soon. May I just touch my son's little cheek?" I ask.

But the doctor takes no notice of my request.

The lady doctor looks me directly in the eye and says, "Nothing has changed with your son. The situation is the same."

I see that Charlie reaches into his pocket and offers the lady doctor two stacks of bills, clearly twice the previous amount. "Here, we want you to have this." The money hangs in the air between them.

"I cannot." The doctor reacts in the same manner as she had earlier. She steps back with one foot, raises her arms, and opens her hands. This time she definitively shakes her head no. "I cannot take any money from you. I have done everything there is to do."

Charlie and I are shocked again. Now I know. She does not believe in the end we will think she deserved it. More money is not going to make a difference. In Romania, most people believe there are few problems money cannot solve. Even when we longed so for a baby, money had made it possible. Dr. Mariana had turned her back on an extraordinary amount of money. I had never seen anyone in Romania turn down money—even money they did not deserve. Charlie looks at me, and we understand this doctor believes there is little hope of Marius's recovery.

CHAPTER 17

Tulcea County Hospital, Tulcea, Romania
August 6, 1991, 4:46 p.m.
Charlie

DR. MARIANA LOOKS ME IN the eyes again, making sure I am intent on her words. "Only God can. Only God, if he desires, can make such a miracle." She quickly turns. Just before she disappears behind the recovery room doors, she turns back and says, "There is nothing more for us to do."

My entire body sinks with the weight of her words. "Only God can?" Who is this god, who may or may not want to make such a miracle? A god bigger than so much money? There is nothing more for me to do? Throughout my whole life, my greatest strength has been my unbeatable effort. I relentlessly persevere. I do not stop. I beat immeasurable obstacles in business and life. And even now at this moment, how many men could have overcome all that has crushed us since Marius fell into the pipe? And now God stands in my way? A god who might or might not want to save this little baby? What kind of god would not save such a sweet little boy?

"Only God can do a miracle," Flori repeats the same words swirling inside my head. "How do we ask God for a miracle?"

I imagine elderly women lighting candles in dark, cold, stone churches.

She repeats my thoughts. "I don't know how to do this. What should we do?"

I disregard her question. "This is only something people say when they cannot think of something to do. Once your aunt gets here, I will drive with Ernest and go back to the hotel. I have more money at the hotel. I will check out and gather our things and get all the money. We may need it in the morning. There will be other doctors."

After looking at my watch, I glance out the window at the parking lot. "I better get out there. They should be arriving and looking for me soon."

CHAPTER 18

Tulcea County Hospital, Tulcea, Romania
August 6, 1991, 4:55 p.m.

CHARLIE GOT TO THE PARKING lot just as Flori's Aunt Cristina and cousin Ernest arrived. It was clear from their expressions as soon as they saw Charlie that Flori's calm voice had not prepared them for what they saw.

"Oh my God! What has happened? Were you in a car accident?" Aunt Cristina cried as she hurried across the narrow strip of parking and up to the door toward Charlie.

"No. Not a car accident." Charlie hugged her and gave her a quick kiss on both cheeks.

"How did you get so bloody?" Aunt Cristina asks.

Charlie began to explain to them as best as he could as they took the elevators up to the second floor. Aunt Cristina rushed to Flori and surrounded her in a hug, many tears, and unanswerable questions. Flori said, "We just need to wash and change clothes, and we can go back in. You can see him then."

Aunt Cristina held up a shopping bag, and she and Flori went into the nearby women's bathroom. They used the paper towels and harsh brown soap to wash Flori's face, arms, and feet. A little bit of lipstick and a hard brush to Flori's dirty hair was all they could do to improve her appearance. The simple white blouse, brown skirt, and a pair of heels completed the transformation adequately. Aunt Cristina tried to tie Flori's hair up, but Flori was out of the door and heading to the medical floor before the ribbon was pulled out of the bag.

Charlie was already in the lobby in one of Ernest's shirts. It was too small for him, but clean, and his face was cleaner, although still wet. They went to the recovery room door and looked for Dr. Mariana. One of the nurses saw them and motioned for them to wait. Almost immediately, the doctor was indicating they could join her at Marius's bedside.

Flori was shocked. Marius lay in the bed unattended. His grossly swollen form lay under a sheet in a big bed, surrounded by people recovering from various operations. The medical staff had not given him any IV fluids or any medication. He was not intubated to provide an airway. Although the oxygen mask was on his face, it remained dark gray. There were no monitors for his heart. Both Charlie and Flori wondered, "Where is there any evidence our son is getting the help we struggled to find?"

Charlie remained at the end of the bed with Ernest, while Flori went right to Marius and touched his cheek. The skin was still cold and had a flat color of light gray. She saw no movement of the chest. His eyes were still swollen closed. Aunt Cristina came up beside Flori. She put her arms behind Flori's back, and they stood in silence for a few minutes.

"Oh, dear, dear little Marius. I had no idea. I thought it was just some small concern of new and overly anxious parents. Flori, Flori." Tears spilled down Aunt Cristina's checks. She moved in closer to the baby, and Flori thought she was going to move in to kiss him. But her hand hesitated above his head, and she did not touch him. Aunt Cristina looked around for a chair. Seeing none, she stood there in silence for several minutes.

"You know, I am a widow, and it was hard for me to raise your cousin. But I prayed to Jesus, and he helped me." Flori looked away from her aunt's most sincere face. Aunt Cristina reached over and pulled back a stray strand of Flori's hair. "You must pray."

Flori looked at her. "I don't know how to pray. Is there a special recipe for a prayer to heal your son?" Flori worried her tone of voice had been too skeptical.

Aunt Cristina didn't seem offended by the tone or question. "No, no Flori. Just call his name, and tell him what you want."

Flori didn't say a word. She did not intend to leave this hospital to go to some dusty, old, empty church to light a candle and mumble a prayer from a printed card.

"Thank you, Aunt Cristina." Flori turned to her aunt, and her aunt put her arms around Flori's shoulders. Flori closed her eyes and did not rush from the embrace. She appreciated that her aunt was offering advice, seeds of hope. Flori knew what she wanted. She wanted her son back as he had been that very morning, laughing and healthy with a long and happy life ahead. She rested her head down on her aunt's shoulder, and the two women gently patted each other on the back, searching for comforting and confirmation that this might all end in a way better than it was at this moment.

Flori sat down on a stool next to the head of the bed. She began to sing Marius a song. It was his favorite song when he was falling asleep. She would sing it softly and slowly rub his back to help him drift off to sleep. But at this moment, all Flori wanted was for him to wake up and breathe.

At quarter after—and at a quarter of each hour—three medical doctors would come to the bedside and listen to his chest and check for a pulse in his arm and neck, look into the closed and distant, locked eyes, and step back. "No change." And they would move on to the next bed.

Those other beds had charts and names, and lots of notations and orders to be heard and initialed. There were none for Marius. No chart, no name on a chart, no list of orders. There was no change, and that seemed to say everything.

Charlie whispered to Ernest, "Dr. Mariana will not take any money. I am not sure what we should do next. It doesn't seem like they are doing much here."

Aunt Cristina overheard Charlie's comment and turned toward Charlie. "A very important supervising doctor for provincial pediatric care lives in an apartment just one floor above me. I know her, and she is most likely at home. Tell her who you are, and ask for her help. Maybe we need the name of another doctor." The men decided to drive over and talk with her.

The drive to the apartment building took less than five minutes, although Charlie, as the passenger, did not keep track of the turns and road names. Ernest, a 27-year-old lawyer, was a good driver. It was a relief to let someone else be in charge and witness competence. Charlie mentally went over his observations of the medical staff's hopelessness. It was something he knew his wife had not allowed herself to understand. The doctors were not aggressively treating Marius to save his life because they did not think there was a life to be saved. They believed all was lost. But none of them would step up and tell that to Flori. Who could speak the words to destroy a mother's determined and confident hope? Or to him, who was confused and frightened, but willing to believe his wife's opinion?

Ernest quickly introduced Charlie and Dr. Helena, who had opened the apartment door. She didn't spend any time listening to his explanation. Her expression and bearing were those of pride and confidence. She looked dismayed at the possible lack of medical urgency that Charlie described. She quickly gathered her bag and locked her apartment door behind her.

The three of them arrived at the hospital shortly, and Dr. Helena asked no one's permission to enter the elevators and head to the pediatric ward. However, Charlie explained Marius was not in the children's department but on the advanced and special care ward on the second floor. The doctor raised her eyebrows. Cocking her head to one side, she did not say anything in response.

It was clear to Charlie from the moment they entered the recovery room and the staff saw Dr. Helena boldly walking down the center aisle that someone of immense influence and authority had arrived. Dr. Mariana greeted her with professional courtesy and then turned to Flori. "Please wait outside while we examine the baby."

The family waited near the elevators. The growing, late-afternoon shadows crept across the floor of the waiting room and then over the worn, brown leather, over-stuffed chairs. The shadows climbed the black and white photographs of the area's flowers.

"Why would they have black and white photographs of such extremely beautiful flowers? Those are bright pink and orange. And the leaves would be an intense green!" Ernest asked no one in particular. So no one answered. They each looked at the six large photographs hanging on the wall. Charlie shrugged. He thought it was a ridiculous question in the darkness of the tragedy they were living. Life had become black and white for Flori and Charlie.

Perhaps fifteen minutes passed. Charlie paced, pausing before a color photograph of one of the trees that grew in the marshes, twisted by the wind but still full of leaves. He just stared at the image, the shadows, and at the angle of each leaf. He knew it was a beautiful photograph, but he also recognized that he was numb to its beauty. He only saw the tree's struggle to survive.

Flori stared out the window. She tried to imagine what the new doctor was finally ordering the staff to do. There must be a lot to do to save a child's life. Most of the time, the four of them spent all their energy beating down the despair that threatened to fill the room. The bitter taste of fear made each swallow almost impossible. No one came out and said, "Your son is dead." But no one came out to say, "He lives." Charlie was holding his breath, waiting for that definitive word. He wondered how long a parent could suffer like this and still survive.

CHAPTER 19

Tulcea County Hospital, Tulcea, Romania
August 6, 1991, about 5:50 p.m.

ALL OF THEM THOUGHT THEY had been waiting for hours, yet when Dr. Helena walked out of the door within fifteen minutes, they were all surprised. The doctor walked over to Ernest and Charlie who stood behind the overstuffed chair into which Aunt Cristina had collapsed. Aunt Cristina reached out for Flori's hand as she moved over and sat on the chair's arm.

"I have heard what they have done for your son. They have done everything in their power to do. Everything possible has been done. We have the nurses coming to bring you some pills to help you. They can do nothing more for your baby." She looked directly into Charlie's eyes. "You understand. There is nothing more to do. They have done all they could. But if I can do something for you, they will call me, and I will return. I have told them you are my friends, and I want you to be cared for as such. But I can do no more for your baby than they have already done."

A young nurse stepped forward and held out a tray with two small white cups, each containing two pills. The supervising director turned and motioned for Dr. Mariana to join her. They did not wait for an elevator but quickly opened the stairway door and were gone. Neither parent reached for the pill cups. The nurse, not certain what to do, remained standing with the pills and the glasses of water. Flori approached her. "They said we could go in and see our son."

The young nurse looked confused. "I will ask." She started to turn toward the ward's door, hesitated, and looked at the pills for Charlie and Flori. She shrugged and walked across the waiting room and through the doors. She never returned with an answer or the pills.

"Come, Flori, let's put some cold water on your face and wash your hands again before you go back in to see Marius." Aunt Cristina led Flori to the ladies' bathroom.

Alone in the hallway, Charlie reached deep into his pocket. There were the first two stacks of folded bills, and now he pulled out all he had with him. He looked down and wondered what to do. Then he saw Dr. Mariana had returned from walking the Superintendent to the main entrance and was opening the recovery doors to return to the patients. Charlie caught up with her and put his hand on the doorframe.

"Dr. Mariana, please, we want you to have this. We want you to take it." There was an enormous amount of cash in his hand, perhaps more than a doctor's yearly government salary. Charlie stepped forward and pressed it down into Dr. Mariana's hand.

Again, Dr. Mariana pulled her hand away and stepped back. "No, no. I cannot take your money. We have done everything we can do. The situation has not changed. There is nothing we can do. Only he can do it." Her open, empty hands came up to her face. "Only God can do such a miracle." She abruptly turned and opened the doors against the force of Charlie's arm. She quickly disappeared behind the recovery room doors.

Charlie felt a weight on his chest, and it became more difficult to take a deep breath. He sat down, and the pressure began to build in his chest and head. Breathing became more and more labored. The room seemed to darken. And a strange sensation causes the room and voices to fade away. He was both in the room and in a distant place. He felt as though he were drowning. There was an overwhelming tightness in his chest, causing him to struggle for each breath.

He closed his eyes to try to stop the sensation. It was paralyzing. It was cold. It was lonely in a terrifying way. Even with his eyes closed, vividly he could still see a small circle of light above and the dark silhouette of two small sticks floating out of his reach. He desperately wanted to escape. "Even if I could reach that stick, how could there be any hope in that small stick?" But there was no sound, no other light, and no other place to look. "Even if I reach that stick, it will not save me."

Charlie's strength and pride drained out of him. Nothing flooded in to fill the space. He understood, for the first-time, that merit, influence, and accomplishments were of little value in this struggle. He was empty, and he knew he had nothing to offer God. He had nothing with which to negotiate, nothing but his lost and empty self. Charlie's eyes were closed, but unexpected sunlight suddenly moved across the water's surface. The vision remained of the sticks floating above and out of reach, but now the light warmed him.

"God, please give my son back." It was Charlie's most personal and genuine prayer of his life. His brain was as broken as his heart. He could not think of fancy words or impressive sentences. Those words were all he had. But he felt the change. God, a god he did not know, heard him beyond his words. And all the empty spaces were filled. His circumstances and the situation had not changed, but he was strengthened in a way that would take a long time to understand.

"If you hear me, please let my son live." A second wave of peacefulness washed over Charlie's mind. He was no longer wrestling to find the next thing to do.

Flori and Aunt Cristina returned. Ernest, who had witnessed Dr. Mariana refuse the gift of money, repeated the story to them with amazement. No one turned down money.

Charlie looked over at Flori and saw she was not devastated by this refusal. Her belief that Marius would live was not based on the unbelievable situation they faced. This new, unexplainable peace now allowed him to believe their son would live. He knew it didn't make sense to anyone else, but he also knew it was the truest thought in the room.

Dr. Lady Mariana, which is what Flori had nicknamed her out of respect and observation of her royal bearing, said, "There has been no change since you first arrived. But you may stay and see."

Flori quickly opened the door and walked down the aisle and returned to Marius's bedside. Charlie followed and stood at the end of the bed. Marius was still badly swollen, but perhaps not quite so much in his face. The color hadn't changed, and he looked smaller in the adult bed than Charlie remembered.

Charlie began to see the nurses looking over at them occasionally. He could tell by their expressions, and the way they never made eye contact, that he and Flori had become the problem to solve. They were the wealthy, influential parents who did not see what was so clear to everyone else. From the moment they had brought the baby into the hospital, there was nothing the medical staff believed could have been done. There was not a sound from the little tube that brought oxygen to Marius's face. No IV or any other treatment was administered. What could they do for the poor, little boy who died on such a lovely summer day?

And so Charlie and Flori watched all the activity around them. Nurses were handing out medication, taking blood samples, marking doctors' orders on charts. Food was brought in on trays, and patients ate. Someone laughed near the doors, and others were talking quietly. Clean, white, sterile pads replaced bandages, and everyone was purposefully busy. No one approached Marius's bed with any treatment or care.

Flori looked around at all this essential medical treatment. "Isn't there something you can do?" she asked Dr. Mariana as the quarter hour exam visit ended.

"Only God can make a miracle." Dr. Mariana looked up. Flori's eyes followed hers up to the ceiling. The ceiling was old with cracks that raced across the room like branches of an ancient tree. Flori wondered how such a smart and accomplished woman continued to be so kind, and yet did not have anything more to offer.

Within ten minutes, Dr. Mariana came over again. "You should leave and take care of yourselves. There is no reason to wait here. There is nothing to do."

Flori shook her head and then rested it on the pillow next to Marius's head. She closed her eyes. She could still smell the stench of the pipe water.

"Okay, if the mother wants to stay at the bedside, we will allow her to as long as she needs to, in spite of the regulations. It is okay, and we will allow it." Turning to Charlie, she said, "But you need to take care of yourself. Tomorrow, your wife is going to need you to be very strong. You are going to need to be strong. You need to eat and rest."

For others on the floor, the drama unfolding with the young family made them hesitate to complain or count their own troubles. To see a young mother suffer as she watched over her baby was unbearable. When the patients asked if something could be done, the nurses shook their heads and silently mouthed, "Nothing." Patients strained to see the baby, or they turned away and did not want to see.

But Charlie now had peace that did not rely on what he saw, for he did not see any life in their baby son, but he believed Marius would live. And for now, their son was not suffering.

Wherever their son was between life and death, his struggle was not with pain. There was no labored breathing or coughing. He did not toss or turn. He was without breath or any sign of life, but no one had outright challenged their belief.

However, Charlie could begin to see the toll this struggle was taking on Flori. There was pain in every muscle, from her fingers which twitched and repeatedly touched Marius's face or chest, to the small muscle in her face that lowered her eyebrows. She whispered to her son, singing favorite songs and adjusting the blankets. Charlie looked at her and wondered what would happen next.

Two doctors across the room worried Charlie. They looked over frequently and then held up patient charts to hide their whispering. Charlie felt Dr. Mariana's attitude was respectful. But some of the other doctors avoided all eye contact and seemed impatient.

The wards' routine was impressive. Marius and other critical patients were visited four times each hour. Two doctors came to the bed on the hour and half-hour examination, and another two would visit at quarter of, and quarter after, each hour. During their visits to Marius, the doctors stood on each side the bed, and each listened to his heart and tried to find a pulse. They would all check for signs of reactions by running a pen across his foot and blowing in his eyes.

They shook their heads and always carefully used the same words, "There is no change." They did not write any notations on a chart that did not hang at the foot of the bed. There had not been one moment of encouragement.

Charlie began to worry how long the force of their own hope could ward off these medical observations. Yes, his wife would need him to be strong, but he wondered what would even be left of Flori to hold close if the doctors came over and tried to pronounce their son dead. Charlie thought she might just disappear. And he also wondered if that wouldn't be what she would desire.

What would happen to him if they then tried to take their son away? Would he fade into vapor, or would he want to fight? Should they try to find another hospital, another doctor? He knew of no better place to go. What does hope look like when it explodes?

CHAPTER 20

On the Road Back to Pelican Resort
August 6, 1991, 6:15 p.m.
Charlie

DR. MARIANA'S EYES PLEAD WITH me to understand. She wants me to rest so that I can be strong tomorrow for Flori. I sense she will not try to tell Flori the bad news if I am not at her side. If pronouncing Marius dead is the doctor's intention, it will not happen until I return.

"You must go and rest so you can return." The doctor's arm on my shoulder was insistent.

"Yes, all right," I agree. I lean over Flori and quietly share. "I need to go back and check out of the hotel. We may need the money that is there."

"Okay, hurry. We cannot go back there." Flori does not look up but continues to nod her head in agreement, and pat my hand that rests on her shoulder.

"Yes. Your aunt will stay with you. Ernest and I will go. We will hurry."

"I will be here." Flori does not smile, but she is more peaceful. The entire medical staff is bustling around her, and she is not struggling with their lack of attention. She strokes Marius's forehead and begins to sing to him again.

I know where I am going, so I drive. It is comforting to do something I am in control of and relaxed doing. Breathing the fresh, early evening air also helps clear my thinking. Ernest asks me how my business is going. I wonder if he thinks talking about something else is good for me. And maybe it is. We talk a little about when I was a driving instructor under the Communist government, and how I taught many officials, celebrities, wealthy businessmen, and their families to drive. These contacts and references had immediately provided a new driving school with substantial clients. After the revolution, I jumped at the chance to open my own business.

I had chosen a business partner who enjoyed the classroom responsibilities and the necessary office routines. The new government continued to require a strict, comprehensive, thirty-hour class and then road experience even before a student attempted to take the test and get a driving license. So, we built the necessary "classroom roadway" since unlicensed drivers could not practice on public streets, and we had been exceptionally successful. Ernest asks questions and seems interested. It is easy to talk about politely, but without too much enthusiasm.

We keep the windows down, and everything around us seems normal. My anguish in the hospital has surprisingly faded, and I smell the fragrant air change, as we near the Danube, from sweet to spicy. The forty-five-minute ride seems so much quicker now that time is less relevant. The road ahead has a sharp curve, and trees line up like soldiers on one side. I recognize the shoulder's wider spot and pull into the grassy area. The scene is surreally calm and beautiful. How could everything return to normal, not even leaving a ripple? There isn't even the slightest indication of Marius's accident.

The campers are setting up chairs near the fire pit. Flames twist around thin spires of smoke, and someone is singing a love song. Near the pipe, we find the folding table closed and the chairs folded and laid down next to it. Flori's and my sandals are right where they randomly fell when we first got up to hunt for Marius. Someone tidied up the remains of the cantaloupe. I glance numbly at these abandoned remnants of our former lives. Flori and I had been here laughing and eating melon a lifetime ago. There isn't even an echo of Marius's laughter. Silently I begin to go over to the pipe, and Ernest follows. I knee down and touch the ground.

"No, that is impossible! It is too small!" Ernest exclaims.

What is there to say? I just nod and point emphatically, indicating it is this pipe.

"No, no, you must be confused. There must be another." Ernest begins looking around the grass.

"No, this is the one."

The campers have seen our car and begin to hurry across the field, arriving just in time to hear Ernest trying to convince me I am mistaken, and the pipe is too small.

"No, he is right. This is the pipe."

"We thought it is too small also, but it is from this pipe that he pulled his son."

"It is true. We saw it with our own eyes."

"How is your baby? How is he doing?"

"He is in the hospital. He is alive." I do not smile.

Everyone reacts genuinely surprised. Someone in the back says, "I thought he was dead. I am surprised to hear this good news that he is at the hospital."

The older man hugs me and shakes his head, smiles, and says, "Good, good. I thought it was impossible to get him out. I don't know how you did it."

Several point up to heaven. "This is unbelievably good news!"

Ernest quietly says, "It is a very serious situation still."

The older man looks at Ernest and soberly agrees, "Oh, yes. We understand. We saw the boy."

I am still kneeling at the pipe. They are kind enough to understand it is not a time for questions or talk, and they become very quiet. Even in my imagination, I cannot believe something as awful as this accident could happen in such a beautiful place. It had been such an amazing morning.

How did we find him in this pipe submerged in the water? I wonder. It would have been easy to miss. There is no little circle of light now. The picture of the little curls slowly floating to the surface breaks through my consciousness and brings the taste of adrenaline and terror into my mouth. I try to take a deep breath, but the air is full of the smell of the hole. I choke on stifled sobs. Again, I go over the unbelievable events. How did we get him out? How did we find him here? I jump to my feet and sternly tell Ernest, "This will not end with Marius's dying. No, he will live."

Once on the road, neither of us speak. If I begin to cry, maybe I won't stop. Maybe I should have waited until morning to return to the resort, but we quickly complete the transaction with few details of the accident.

Long, golden shadows dabble the road. The light intensifies the colors of the grass and the blue Danube water, and these became the canvases for silhouettes of trees and flocks of flying birds. How could such an awful day end in such majesty? We both see the scarlet sky but silently drive into the early twilight until I turn on our headlights.

CHAPTER 21

Tulcea County Hospital, Tulcea, Romania
August 6, 1991, about 7:20 p.m.

AT THE HOSPITAL, FLORI CONTINUED to sit on a small stool so her face could be near Marius's. She tried to rest, closing her eyes and breathing slowly. She had been somewhat relieved when Aunt Cristina had left just before seven-fifteen. Since Flori couldn't concentrate on what people were saying, she was relieved to be alone.

She could not hear any oxygen being pumped by the tank into her baby's lungs. But somehow, concentrating on her own rhythmic breathing seemed to comfort her that Marius was getting what he needed, in spite of the lack of medical attention. She placed first her right and then her left hand firmly on his chest. She closed her eyes.

Suddenly a violent convulsion seized Marius's body. It looked as though a strong electrical shock surged through him. His back arched up, and his body became rigid. He shook with after-shocks.

Flori stood up and screamed, "I need help!" She was horrified that the little body was being racked so violently. It was only the second time she had seen her son move, and she knew it would bring medical attention.

The doctors in the room rushed to the bedside. The first thing they did was to remove the oxygen mask. And then they listened to his chest.

"No, there is still no heartbeat." The doctor said this in a loud, emphatic, voice that seemed to echo in the room.

Flori began to massage Marius's legs and arms as she had done in the ambulance. She hoped it would help the muscles relax and allow him to lie easily in the bed. The others just stood at the bedside and watched. Flori panicked, and she followed her instinct to climb on top of her son and have her weight press against his arched body in a maternal hug. This shocked the nurses, and one of them yelled, "Lady, stop! What are you doing?"

Dr. Mariana was quickly at the bedside. No one administered any medical help. "Let her do whatever she needs to do. She is this baby's mother." The nurses and doctor watched as Flori continued to cling to her son. Slowly the small, rigid body softened and rested back on the bed.

Once the convulsion passed, Flori rolled over and stood beside the bed. The doctor listened again with her stethoscope, and once again she shook her head indicating no heartbeat. Another doctor ran the pen against the inside of the baby's palm and the bottom of his foot. There were no reactions. The doctors all looked at each other and seemed to indicate they all agreed. No one wrote any notes on the nameless chart.

The older doctor looked over at Flori. His eyes ask flatly, "Don't you see what has happened to your son? You need to wait for more?" The doctor removed the oxygen tank's mask and reached over and turned off the valve at the tank. Flori did not say a word to them. She purposely did not look them in the eyes. Flori was exhausted. What could she say to these doctors who saw no reason for even oxygen? She sank down on the stool.

"Jesus, I do not give you my son." And to her baby son, she pleaded, "You must give me a sign now. Do something! Move, cough, cry! Show them you are alive. We cannot wait much longer." She could sense there was growing pressure to move Marius from the room. She suspected some had begun to talk of him as a corpse. She could feel the pressure to prove he would live.

Someone offered Flori a sedative again, and she refused. She sat on the stool and placed one hand on Marius's heart and the other on his stomach, and then she half-draped her body over his. No one came to the bed, but she was holding her territory. No one was going to take him anywhere. She tensely sat guard so no one would attempt.

Once Charlie and Ernest arrived back in the city, Ernest was dropped off at his mother's apartment. Charlie expected the hospital perhaps had moved Marius over to the pediatric section. When he inquired at the desk, the nurse had said Marius and Flori were in the same ward and bed because the doctors didn't want to upset the parents of other children. Charlie thought it was a very odd thing to say, and he wondered what it meant. He had not been encouraged by it.

He came in and saw Marius looked the same. There had not been any change or improvement in his coloring. No doctor had heard a heartbeat or felt a pulse. There had been the convulsion, but no other body movement. In fact, he saw just the opposite of improvement as Marius's skin was dull and lacked elasticity and warmth. Charlie couldn't say anything. He took Flori into his arms and just held her. Above her head, he bit his lips not to cry out. He could feel himself beginning to shake, so he pulled away. He did not want Flori to know he was struggling not to cry. She looked so tired, but still stronger than he felt.

Flori had seen Charlie coming down the center aisle, and she was overwhelmed with relief. In his arms, she felt safe from the guilt building in her chest. She was the mother, and it had been her job to judge the situation and protect Marius. Charlie's strong arms around her strengthened her. He looked into her eyes, and all that could not be said was understood. He did not condemn her—he loved her. He was not thinking of blaming her. He wanted to comfort her.

He went to the other side of the bed and sat down. She sat again on the stool. Their eyes met and then looked down at their son. Flori wrapped a curl around her finger. Charlie kissed his ear and neck. Their fingers interlocked over Marius's heart.

Since the baby had arrived, patients well enough to notice had strained to see who was at the bedside and what the problem was. Many saw the skin's gray color and age of the patient, and compassionately felt the anguish of the young parents. It had been too much to share, and some had turned and tried not to think about it. Others had followed along, watching each visit from the doctors, hoping there would be an improvement, and sharing disappointment when nothing changed. Most had just been confused about why such a gravely ill child was there and not getting more help.

At around eleven-thirty, Doctor Mariana arrived with two other younger doctors for another examination, and Charlie went to the end of the bed to make room for them. He braced himself for what they would say. Each doctor, in turn, listened for Marius's heartbeat. Each listened intently, carefully. Then one by one they shook their heads no. Not one of them had heard a heartbeat. There was no respiration. There was no response to a pen run along the bottom of the foot. There was no response when each carefully lifted a tiny eyelid surrounded by dark, long lashes and blew into his eye.

"No change."

The doctors moved on to the next bed of a critical patient. Charlie breathed out a long breath. They had been given another fifteen minutes to sit at their son's bed before the next exam.

CHAPTER 22

Tulcea County Hospital Tulcea, Romania
August 6, 1991, about 11:30 p.m.
Flori

I AM EXHAUSTED AND SIT on the little stool. It gives me a close-up look at Marius's face. Now I can look at his almost unrecognizable face, with distorted coloring and swollen features. In fact, I cannot take my eyes off of him. He doesn't look like my baby, but we are here together. Rounds are completed, and the lights lowered. Patients drift off to sleep. I am surrounded by soft snoring, and familiar names whispered in the sleep-filled darkness.

"Can you get me a glass of water?" an older woman across the aisle asks Charlie.

Charlie is startled and jumps. He looks over at the woman. And I can see he is wondering why she asked him to get her a glass of water. It is a simple request, but our minds are filled with bigger problems. I know my husband, and he is annoyed that she would ask.

"A glass of water?" he asks.

"Yes, please," she repeats.

I think he might say no, but the woman is very old, so I encourage him, "Yes, Charlie, it is over there. They will give you a glass." I motion to the end of the row of beds where water is available. Charlie looks at me, and I smile and nod a little more encouragement.

Charlie shrugs his shoulders. "Yes, of course."

Charlie successfully pours the water and brings it back to the woman. I am surprised that Charlie is more than polite. He is being kind to the woman and says something that makes the woman smile. I am pleased he seems to have it under control. I turn back to look at Marius.

Marius's eyes are open!

A dream? A vision? Is this possible? I don't move for fear of changing the magic of the moment. My son is looking gently into my eyes. They are Marius's eyes, wide open and full of curiosity, warmth, and charm.

I hold my breath. Can I trust my eyes? Or is this only my heart's desire for hope?

Marius's left hand reaches out. I blink. Will I feel his touch, or would it burst this dream? His hand slowly continues to move toward my face, and then I feel his warm, little finger touch my lips, gently tracing the outline of my nose to the top lip and back up. He reaches out and grabs my necklace, just as he has done a hundred times. There is a shudder in my chest.

"Mommy," my son whispers softly with a smile.

Then his eyes close.

I am stunned silent. I cannot even trust what I have seen. Perhaps I have gone crazy, and it was a hallucination.

But his body is not rigid. It is relaxed, and his chest is moving up and down. Marius's color is returning to pink. He is no longer swollen, and yet his little body increases, taking up space with movement and sound. Where once his small limp, swollen body had seemed to be lost in the sheets, now it has a shocking living presence. He is sleeping. His eyes are closed because he is sleeping.

I stand up in shocked belief, knocking down the stool. Charlie is returning from helping with the water. I look at him and shout, "He is alive! My baby is alive! He has come back to life!"

CHAPTER 23

Tulcea County Hospital, Tulcea, Romania
August 6, 1991, about 11:35 p.m.
Charlie

FLORI SURPRISES ME WHEN SHE jumps up and knocks over the stool. The clang echoes in the quiet ward. But then she doesn't get quieter, but louder! She screams that Marius is alive and he has come back to life! I look first at her and then at our son in the bed. It is immediately true to my deepest level of understanding. Marius's skin is changing from flat, cold, gray to warm, pink, living flesh. But it is so much more than color. In front of my eyes, I watch the muscles transforming and shaping Marius's baby's body from death to life. The limpness and stillness, and even silence of death, are giving way to movement and breath, heartbeat and substance. It is, in an instant, both a complete and unwavering understanding of what I have not accepted—my son's death—to a complete and unwavering knowledge that Marius is now alive. I am astonished by the enormity of both ideas—what I had not understood, and now what I do understand. Both are unbelievable, and both are completely true. In seeing life, I am convinced that I saw death. It is all incomprehensible and all true.

"It is true! It is true! He is breathing!" I shout back to Flori and the world. I throw my arms around Flori, and we embrace and emit sounds that alternate between laughter and relief. I have never made sounds like those, nor has Flori, but they come freely without embarrassment. My toes cannot remain on the floor, and I begin to jump and leap down the center aisle.

"Marius is alive! He is breathing!"

CHAPTER 24

Tulcea County Hospital, Tulcea, Romania
August 6, 1991, about 11:40 p.m.

THE OTHER BEDS WERE FILLED with patients who were now straining to see what was happening. They began to sit up and ask questions. And some were struggling to get up and pull their IV poles along to see what was going on. The seriousness of the baby's condition had not been lost on the other patients. The baby had neither moved nor cried, and that had been deeply disturbing to them.

Now the tall father was jumping and running and laughing with his hands above his head, and shouting his son was alive! Was it true or was the man crazy with grief? Their own suffering or weakness made it all the harder to understand. Some patients did get up and pushed or pulled IV poles over toward the bed. They saw a sleeping child, looking no different from one of their own children or grandchildren taking a nap. And these patients began to cry out and hug each other, and also hug Flori and Charlie. A huge ripple of energized joy began to float across and down the rows of beds. The patients became like one family, understanding that something extraordinary had happened in their presence.

Weak patients struggled to get out of bed and walk toward the child. Sleeping patients woke, smiled, and quickly joined others until the whole room was rejoicing and singing out in joy.

All this activity and noise quickly got the attention of the doctors and nurses who were in an office just outside the doors. Doctor Mariana saw Charlie running around, picking up patients and shouting his son had come to life. She ran down the center aisle and around the patients who were now out of bed and pushing forward to be closer to the child and parents.

"There! There now. Calm down. Be quieter. Look at what you have caused." She was swept up in Charlie's hug and swung around. She patted his back with her hands and tried to hold his arms firmly down. "Shhhhhh now, it will all be all right."

Flori called over the crowd, "He opened his eyes and said, 'Mommy!'"

The doctor looked around to see if there were other doctors or nurses nearby who would help her gain control of these parents. Maybe she had made a mistake in the way she had tried to handle them. Denial had given way to hysteria. Gently pushing aside all the patients in the aisle, a doctor and nurse were also trying to make their way to Marius's bed. Dr. Mariana gave them a silent head nod asking them to help her control Charlie. Then a woman sat down on the bed next to Marius's. This gave Doctor Mariana her first direct and unobstructed view of the baby.

Dr. Mariana's eyes widened, and her body shuddered with shock. Immediately she let out an uncontrolled, loud scream. She continued pushing through the patients and arriving nurses, screaming louder than Charlie. There was the baby, full of breath and life—the color of his skin moist and pink. His legs were moving gently, and his breathing lifted the sheets covering his chest.

"God! Oh, God! He is alive!" Doctor Mariana shouted, "Only God could do this! Only God could make a miracle like this! This child was dead, and now he is alive!" And Dr. Lady Mariana took two steps back, and then three toward the bed. She started jumping and laughing and praising God with both of her hands above her head.

More nurses arrived, and they saw the baby and the doctor, and they couldn't understand all they saw. But Doctor Mariana was pacing up and down the aisle. She was shouting to the parents, "We had only kept him here for you. For you! We only were trying to take care of you!" Doctor Mariana continued wildly, moving her hands from her heart to her head and back. "I am a medical doctor, and I know what death looks like—and this baby was dead!"

The nurses both became pale and frightened. The younger began to cry, "It is true what the doctor says. We did not admit the baby. We did nothing for him." But on seeing the doctor in a dance of mysterious joy, they too began to hug each other and cry. Everyone was hugging and dancing or laughing or crying. Even those too ill to stand were sitting up and joining the joyful chorus.

Doctor Mariana's emotional response stunned Charlie. She had been so calm and professional. He had seen her expression when she entered the medical ward, and he knew she was marching in to calm and quiet him. But here she was making even a louder and greater commotion. He had not expected the doctor to announce so loudly, and definitively, that Marius had been dead. Although in some way he had observed there was no breath or heartbeat, he had been certain their baby would live. It had been more than denial because it hadn't been born in fear, but in a calm peace that overrode the reality of everything he saw. But here was their doctor, who had not once said Marius was dead, screaming God had made a miracle and a dead baby was now alive.

Charlie grabbed her and began to pat her back and reassure her, "There, there, it will be all right." He laughs loudly.

Doctor Mariana looked him in the face and said, "You do not understand. No, you do not understand. We do not see this. God! God gave you your son two times. God did this for you. I did nothing. There was nothing I could do for your baby. God did this for you. Go to church and bring your thanks to God!"

And then the doctor rushed to the bedside to touch this living miracle. She listened to Marius's chest. "His heart is strong and steady." She took the pen and ran it against the bottom of his foot. The boy pulled back, and his toes curled in. "Yes, again perfect!"

Flori watched the toes react and shuddered. She, for the first time, began to understand in a completely new way all the lifelessness she had witnessed four times each hour. Days later, she would think back to the revelation she had not missed Marius's life until she saw it return in so many ways. How could it be she was now so completely overcome with this life-joy and had not earlier been in an equal measure overcome by death? But in each person's life, there are moments of such utter happiness there is nothing to do but give in to the experience without question or examination.

This experience of extraordinary joy filled everyone in the room. There was a bubbling and dancing, not only inside each heart but also between hearts. Joy in one multiplied joy for seven persons nearby. Minds and spirits soared in the swirling clouds that were the indescribable colors of blessings and grace! And there was no effort needed to sustain this flight, nor any need for it to land and rest. Hope had exploded in an entirely unexpected way. And nothing any of them had ever experienced or enjoyed—neither northern lights, first snowfalls, flowers blossoming, sunsets, brides nor newborn babies—could be compared to this joy. Death had become life.

Some people would, much later, remember and long for these emotions and comfort when they stood at the grave of one whom they loved. They would hope that waiting on the other side of death, unseen by human eyes, was this same indescribable joyful celebration: death transformed into life. Many patients, nurses, and doctors who had the night shift would try to explain how such a brief experience had convinced their souls of such a hope. It was easier to share just the details of the story. For some, it would remain a personal, emotional retreat during difficult times. They would be strengthened beyond what they could see.

Amidst all this excitement, a nurse was instructed to put Marius's name on the outside of a chart hanging on the foot of the bed. Now orders for blood tests were being given and dutifully written inside. An IV was inserted, and arrangements were being made to move the child to a private room prepared for important or wealthy patients. "Now he is alive, there is much we can do!" Dr. Mariana had exclaimed when she had switched from shock to practical. "Let's carefully go over all that happened and determine how long your son was submerged! Now I can be his doctor!"

CHAPTER 25

Tulcea County Hospital, Tulcea, Romania
Near midnight to the morning of August 7, 1991

FIRST, ANOTHER TANK OF OXYGEN was substituted, and then a mask was placed around Marius's face. Flori asked, "Why don't you use the tank at the head of the bed?"

The nurse explained, "There isn't enough pressure or even much oxygen in that tank. The doctors only had us bring that in so you would stop asking for it."

Flori had been shocked by the comment, but she looked at her son sleeping. She had nothing to complain about now. The adorable faces he made in his sleep charmed her again. What were his dreams that brought a little smile to his lips, or made his eyes dart back and forth under his eyelids? She had missed them so much. His little, left arm and hand with gentle fingers reached up and above his head. He stretched and arched his back and then collapsed into a peaceful slumber.

Charlie sat next to the other side of the bed and picked up this small hand. Marius's fingers wrapped around Charlie's large thumb. They both saw it, and at the same time, the memory of Marius's hand in the pipe when it could not grab his father's fingers flooded into every cell of their bodies. Now feeling Marius's warm fingers firmly grasp his own touched Charlie deeply, and he placed his face on the pillow and cried without embarrassment or restraint. Flori reached over first to Marius's head and then Charlie's hands and gently patted

90

them as if to say, "We are here. We are all here together, and we are all safe." She placed her head on the pillow and wept also.

Soon the new nurses were there with a bigger oxygen tank, and a new mask that they placed over Marius's sleeping face. Soon Marius was quickly transferred on a stretcher to another floor. The new room had a special youth-sized bed, and chairs were brought in for them. Although of average size and modestly furnished, the private room was reserved for elite political or influential patients. There was no number on the door. Everyone knew the room and its importance. There was also a second bed, and they were permitted to stay and sleep.

The dramatic change in medical attention and care created a busy, professional scene. Several nurses quickly dictated and transcribed vital statistics of heart rate, respiration, and body temperature. Doctors explained their orders to nurses and other hospital staff involved in Marius's care. A chart was brought in to hang at the end of his bed, and the young nurse wrote his name with a marker on the admission page. Flori gasped when she saw Marius's name written so boldly; it was a statement of his presence and existence in the world again.

Marius was finally officially admitted to Tulcea County Hospital. Orderlies brought in more large tanks of oxygen. A team of hospital workers brought in poles with hanging IV bags, and staff members followed with extra medical supplies from the room's cabinet.

"Now there is so much we can do. We can take care of your son now." Doctor Mariana was at the center of the unfolding drama of excitement and attention. Although her shift should have ended at midnight, she stayed and was clearly in charge. She supervised every order, and everyone understood the need for the best care and careful observation.

"I have ordered the lab to stay open and to complete these blood and urine tests by the morning. All of the observations we have from our examinations are normal. He has a normal pulse rate, temperature, and lung sounds. His movements and cognitive evaluations support that he is not in a coma. He is sleeping." The doctor paused, her shoulders dropping in a relaxed attitude. She looked up into their eyes, and she smiled. "He is just sleeping."

Flori and Charlie hugged each other and embraced the doctor. They all took deep breaths and wiped tears from their faces. Within a minute, the doctor shifted back into a professional mode.

"Thank you, Dr. Lady Mariana," Flori said.

"No, God did this! You must thank him." Dr. Mariana looked as seriously at the parents as she ever had. Her eyes demanded a response.

Flori and Charlie agreed, "Yes, we will."

Doctor Mariana paused and looked down at her chart and continued, "However, I need to prepare you to expect this will be a bumpy road. When you first looked into the pipe, and your son was not visible and submerged, how much time passed until you successfully pulled him out?"

They paused and then replied in unison, "Six minutes, maybe a bit more."

Dr. Lady Mariana continued, "Okay, if we include the time it took you to find the pipe, we believe Marius was submerged at least eight minutes." She paused, and she slowly shook her head. Then the doctor turned back and looked them in the eyes. "We will have setbacks and have to fight the infections that will follow with his lungs' exposure to such dirty water. There was a lot of algae in the water. I expect he will run fevers that might be high. We will see." Dr. Mariana looked at them most sincerely and tilted her head. "At least eight minutes submerged. More than seven hours here. Oh, my God."

What Dr. Mariana did not share was the latest medical understanding of the process of drowning. A person can hold his breath until he is forced to take a breath. Then water rushes into the mouth and induces spasms of the larynx. This closes the trachea to protect the lungs, resulting in little water entering the lungs. This reflex also results in a significant reduction of oxygen to the lungs and thus into the blood. This lack of oxygen, anoxia, affects the brain within thirty seconds. The brain begins to fail. The person then inhales and aspirates water into the lungs before a new spasm closes the trachea again, but this time for a shorter duration. With each new inhalation, more water is aspirated, and there is a shorter duration before the next inhalation.

This pattern continues. During this time the person's blood is infused with water, and the blood's ability to deliver oxygen to the body decreases, leading to a loss of consciousness. Death from drowning occurs quickly, often in two minutes or less, but quicker in warm water and with children. Once a person is unconscious, the body sinks. Fat bodies are slightly more buoyant than thin bodies—but still, all bodies will sink in fresh water. If the person is wearing clothing along with shoes, the body is considerably less buoyant. The doctor thought it was just too much to explain and too much she could not explain. How could this baby be alive and be so perfectly well?

Her eyes met theirs. She did not blink. "You must thank God for your son to be given back to you."

"Yes, of course, doctor."

"We do not know what damage might follow. There may be paralysis. We can treat all of this. Your son may seem different for a while, not have the same cognitive ability or speech, but we will have to wait to see how much he will improve. It will take years to reach his optimum recovery. I want to examine him carefully now."

Marius was still asleep as the doctor's gentle fingers started examining the soft tissue and bones of his neck. She checked his shoulders and listened to his chest.

"Amazingly perfect. I do not hear any rattling or mucus in his lungs. He has normal breath sounds."

Flori smiled. Charlie put his hand on her shoulder and squeezed gently.

The doctor continued the examination with Marius's neck. She gently moved his head to the left and right. Then she did the same, forward and backward. She examined the left side of his head. And then she repeated the careful examination of the right side. Finally, she sat Marius up and rocked his sleeping body over her left arm to get a good look at the back of his head.

They were all shocked to see a large wound. "What? What is this on the top of his head? Had you seen this?" Doctor Mariana asked.

"No! No," Flori and Charlie both repeated.

Marius's head had a large gash. The skin was broken, and the two-inch head wound looked like a significant scrape. The scalp was opened and peeled down. At the top of the wound was a perfectly round, two-inch circle. Only a little red blood now oozed from the edges of the wound. There were no bruises.

"There wasn't any blood. I held him. There wasn't any bleeding or blood," Flori said.

"No, we didn't know," Charlie added.

"Okay, in the other room we did not see any blood on the pillow. We will have a head X-ray today. We will put this on our list to do today." Doctor Mariana finished her examination and gently folded the soft blanket up to the baby's chin.

Softly Flori said, "It didn't bleed. It didn't bleed."

"It was the broom handle," Charlie cried out. "The wound is from when I thrust the broom handle into the pipe because I did not believe you, Flori. I used so much force because I was upset. I did this to our son! Look what I have done."

The doctor turned Marius's head to the side and looked at the wound again. Flori could see the top of the wound did look just the same shape and size of the broom handle. Charlie saw it too, and Flori could see the weight of this self-condemnation fall across his chest and soul.

"We need to wait. We will take an X-ray to be sure. He seems to be good and has come through far more dangers than this wound. It doesn't appear to be deep. We will wait and see." The doctor patted Charlie on the arm, and she managed a smile. "Don't worry about what you may not have to worry about. I am staying at the hospital to research similar events. I intend to be at the hospital all night. Have the nurse call me if you wish." Dr. Mariana went to the door, turned and said to Flori, "The heart wasn't beating, so there was no bleeding." She gave them a huge smile and left.

The parade of doctors and nurses continued. Doctors came in and listened to his chest and took his pulse. Each time, numbers and results were written accurately in his chart. Each time, the doctors smiled and encouraged Flori and Charlie with reports that everything seemed normal. "No change" meant an entirely different thing! It was great news. Nurses followed and took his temperature once an hour.

Marius just slept. His little eyes darted behind his almost translucent eyelids as he chased the dreams of toddlers. There were no fitful nightmares. His gentle movements were wonderful to watch. His body was no longer swollen, and his skin was peachy pink. Flori couldn't take her eyes off of her son. She tried not to think of how still and discolored Marius had been just an hour ago. When she did, there was an involuntary physical reaction—a vigorous body shudder, eyes snapped shut, and head pulled back and away.

Charlie tried not to relive the accident and resulting trauma. It was impossible to understand, and he was following the doctor's advice not to worry. However, the sight of the circle wound on the top of his son's head haunted him. Involuntary images of himself thrusting down the broom handle flashed in his mind, complete with imaginary images of it hitting Marius. He thought of his attitude when he lifted it above his head. All of this created a panic, sending adrenalin surges throughout his body. He had to look intentionally to the living hope who now slept peacefully in the small hospital bed to make these experiences stop.

During the early morning hours, Marius's examinations and tests continued. The next hours were filled, as more blood and urine samples were taken along with X-rays of his lungs. By three o'clock in the morning, the flurry of activity had waned. Only an occasional footstep could be heard in the hall. The hospital had finally fallen into the peaceful embrace of night. Charlie looked at the single bed and pushed it over closer to Marius's crib-bed. "Flori, sleep here. You can wake and open your eyes and see your son sleeping near. It is safe for you to sleep. Tomorrow we will need our strength. I will go back to your aunt's apartment, share this good news, and return in the morning."

For the next few hours while Marius slept peacefully, so did Flori. Regularly she stirred when Marius tried to remove the IV, and she would comfort him until he fell back to sleep. Around four-thirty, Flori woke. She was startled by the initial strangeness of her surroundings and the immediate memories of the previous day's horror. She touched him to relax.

However, as soon as Marius woke up, he was intent on taking out the IV and removing the oxygen mask. She helped him get the mask off and made the tubes loose enough for them to snuggle in bed. Flori closed her eyes as she held him close. She smiled at the assurance that Marius had not lost any of his curious energy. Snuggled up together, they both drifted in and out of sleep.

Soon Charlie came back to the hospital. "I could not stay away. I could not go back to sleep. I am so happy." He sat down in the chair and reached out to Flori's hand. Looking her right in the eyes, he said firmly, "I have to leave Romania."

Flori looked at him. He looked fine. He looked normal. Flori's thoughts raced. *Charlie had never once said that he wanted to leave Romania. He might as well have said he wanted to go to the moon. What did he mean? Another vacation? Was he done with the country because of the accident?*

Flori just stared back at him. "What do you mean?"

"I know I need to leave Romania."

"Where do you want to go?"

"I don't know where."

Flori looked at Charlie. What was wrong with him? Why was he bringing this big, life-changing idea to her this morning? She was exhausted; she was overwhelmed with what had happened. What was this? Stress? An emotional breakdown? It was too much for her to deal with. She would get through today. She would face all the possible problems Doctor Mariana had explained to them. She would work through guilt, remorse, and fear. But she could not deal with Charlie's announcement he needed to leave Romania—not right now. If Charlie were going to have a nervous breakdown today, he would have to handle it alone.

She looked over at him as he kissed Marius's fingers and rubbed his toes. Marius was waking up again from a short nap. Charlie looked calm. Yes, she would handle one crisis at a time. Charlie would straighten up and think more clearly as Marius improved.

Once the earliest light of dawn began to fill the room with the day's warmth, Doctor Mariana returned. She had spent the night researching. But no medical examples explained Marius's unique outcome. In light of all she had witnessed, it could not be professionally explained, so she remained cautiously optimistic. Many possible complications were life-threatening, such as pneumonia and renal failure, and even a rare occurrence called "secondary drowning." Symptoms could develop over the course of several days, or even longer for some patients. Marius was a highly unusual patient; he was showing no symptoms or adverse signs of his ordeal.

The sunshine broke through the branches and leaves of the large oak tree growing outside their new room. The tree was large, reaching up at least another story, and the large windows gave the impression their room was part of a tree house. The sunshine made hundreds of little shadows on the walls. Each danced as the leaves moved in the morning breeze. Within ten minutes the sun rose higher on the horizon, and the effect was gone. Marius woke up. The three of them read a book Charlie had found in the car. It was one of Marius's favorites. He remembered each illustration and rhyme. It seemed the most normal of mornings. It was easy to forget everything else.

After a half-hour, Marius wanted to wiggle off the edge of the bed and look around. He began exploring by climbing onto the chair and turning the light on and off. Doctor Mariana arrived at the door just as Marius dragged the IV pole into the middle of the room. It began to tip, and all the adults in the room rushed to stabilize it. Dr. Mariana stopped and stared at this little boy who was a picture of a healthy toddler.

"Mama up. Get up." Marius reached up to Flori to be picked up.

"He is the same! He is talking and awake," Charlie laughed.

Dr. Mariana watched and finally broke into a huge smile. "How can this be? This recovery is as amazing as what happened last night. They both are miracles." She stood at the door and considered what she should do next. She decided to sit down, and Marius immediately walked over to her and touched the stethoscope. He looked into her face and laughed. She laughed back. Perhaps the tests would be unnecessary. Quickly she changed her mind. The situation could not have been more serious, and she should proceed with all caution.

"I am going to share this second miracle with my colleagues! They will not believe me, so expect visitors soon!" She left, and within a few minutes, brought back several other doctors. All of them laughed at Marius's pole-dragging skills. Then Marius answered their questions by pointing correctly to his toes and nose and pointing up and down. He was bright and charming as he sang a favorite song.

The doctors and nurses who flooded into the room were overwhelmed with this boy's unexpected and spectacular recovery. They were used to routine results, to long and difficult recoveries, and to compromised outcomes. They remembered painful, distant moments when the heartbroken tears of families were woven into their own lives. It was the type of work that found its way into personal lives in unwelcomed ways. But here was a child they and many of their co-workers had seen dead, who now was playing and laughing! How was this possible?

But everyone in the hospital wanted to be part of the experience. This was joy they could gather in and hold onto tightly. This moment could be a reservoir of strength to call upon on days that almost broke them. It would make their steps a little faster and lighter, and it made their conversations more animated and playful. So soon the number of doctors, nurses, supervisors, and general staff grew. Some came in, read, checked the chart, and then expressed their disbelief in various ways. They slapped Charlie's back, hugged Flori, played with Marius, and congratulated them all.

Others just peeked in and asked, "Is this the miracle child?" or "He is so cute and healthy. Is this really the one?"

Dr. Mariana arrived at their door again, and she had the district supervisor from the night before with her. "I called Dr. Helena this morning with this amazing news. She came right over!"

They were both smiling. Dr. Helena said, "Is this the same boy I looked at last night? Are you sure you didn't switch him for another?" The doctor was teasing, but the transformation was so complete it would almost be easier to believe there had been a trick than to believe what she saw before her.

"No, no, this is our son. Go and look at Cristina's photographs in her apartment." Charlie smiled back.

"Yes, yes, I believe you—but it is also unbelievable."

Dr. Mariana said, "I have told them all we did last night was to take care of them. There was nothing I could do for Marius." Marius was now attempting to show the doctors his book. The doctor leaned over and lifted him up.

"This is true. I saw the situation myself. There was nothing to do for your son. I am so happy for you and your family. Do you see any change?"

"No, he is the same," Flori declared.

"Well, he is a special one."

Once the supervisor left, Aunt Cristina and Ernest both arrived. Cristina had somewhere found a small stuffed dog, which she gave to Marius. The whole amazing truth was discussed and marveled at all over again. "Flori, your son was dead. And now he is alive. You need to thank God," said Cristina. She continued playing with the little dog and tickling Marius's neck.

Flori heard the word *dead* and was overcome with debilitating exhaustion. Her thoughts slowed to a crawl, and the word *dead* pounded in her head. Guilt assaulted all her senses. *He died, and I am his mother. It was my responsibility to watch and keep him safe*, she thought. Her head throbbed. She got up and sat down on the floor near Marius. Where he walked, she walked. What he touched, she washed in the bathroom sink. Every move and every word he uttered, she over-analyzed and expressed concern. *Was he walking off balance? Had he dropped the toy because his hand was weak? Is he warm and beginning a fever?*

The others in the room saw her sudden intensity and change in behavior. Charlie tried to distract her. He brought her a glass of water and asked if she had eaten. She had not. She was determined to be at Marius's elbow. She was not easily distracted from the holy obsession of mothering.

Aunt Cristina left the room and came back with Dr. Mariana, who quickly took charge. "Flori, you go to bed. Everyone else, please leave. Let's hang a sign on the door—No Visitors. And Charlie, you go with the child to get the head X-ray."

Everyone did as directed, and Flori was alone in the darkened room. Her heart pounded in her chest and ears. Everything seemed wrong, and her arms and hands tingled with tiny needles of sparking pain. The second attack of guilt came in the form of "The What If's." The list was never-ending. What if there was brain damage that showed up later? What if the algae started to grow in his lungs, causing life-threatening infection? What if it happened again? What if something else just as bad happened? At some level, Flori understood the long list of "what if's" was dangerous and destructive. But she couldn't stop them. And then, when she finally went to sleep, they tormented her dreams.

She woke with a fearful start, overheated and sweaty. She had a terrible taste in her mouth. She didn't feel safe yet, and it calmed her to understand she didn't need to relax. It just wasn't over yet. She knew she wasn't afforded the luxury of falling apart. No, not yet. Maybe something else might happen.

CHAPTER 26

Tulcea County Hospital, Tulcea, Romania
August 7, 1991, early afternoon
Flori

MARIUS FINISHES THE LAST SPOONFUL of his lunch, and Charlie eats the apple. Now I am watching the two of them sitting in an over-stuffed chair, looking through a fishing catalog Charlie found in the lobby. Charlie is talking quietly to Marius, who is content to be in his daddy's arms. I need to stop looking for the trouble and see the good. A nurse places an envelope into Marius's chart on the foot of the bed. I cannot help but reach over and pull the envelope from the chart. Cranium X-ray results. The words "cranium fracture" jump from the page. "Open bone fracture is pressing on brain tissue resulting in bleeding. Immediate surgery recommended." I reread the report three times.

"Bring Marius over here, Charlie. Let me look at him."

Charlie has Marius on his shoulders and pretends to dump him onto the second bed with me. Hearing the alarm in my voice, he sees the open report and picks it up to read it while I am busy removing the simple gauze bandage over Marius's head wound. I gently touch it, and Marius doesn't call out in pain. He tries to brush my hand away, but there is no outcry. It looks significant, but it isn't deep. I press harder on the bone underneath the worst area. Marius again doesn't cry out in pain.

"The report is wrong. Charlie, listen to me. This is wrong."

Charlie throws the report and X-rays down on the bed. "What have I done? He escaped the pipe only to have his own father kill him? I killed our son with a broomstick!"

Marius has picked up the toy dog and is trying to make realistic barking sounds. Once he perfects the bark, he becomes the dog, down on his knees and hands, barking up a storm. I grab our squirmy toddler and lift him up to Charlie. "Hold him. I want to check again."

"Charlie, look, it is superficial. It is not a serious wound. Look. There is no sign of such a serious injury. Look at him play. He is not brain damaged in need of surgery."

Unconvinced, Charlie suggests, "Let's call Dr. Mariana and let her examine him."

I stay alert, knowing the world is not safe enough when you love this much. My husband and I spend the day encouraging each other with an appreciation of every adorable thing Marius does. Later in the afternoon, when Dr. Mariana has finished the surgery, she knocks on the door. "I have seen the X-ray. It is just as the report says. A serious condition."

"Dr. Mariana, look at Marius. Does it look like he has such a serious head injury that he needs immediate surgery?" I ask.

"It is a real cut, but it doesn't seem to have injured the bone underneath. I do not see the bone displaced," she says after a careful examination.

Charlie asks, "Is it possible the X-ray has been switched with another child?"

"Yes, not probable. But it is possible. I prefer to X-ray again. Charlie, bring Marius, and we will re-X-ray now. And then you can come back and have your supper, Marius!" She waits for Charlie to pick our son up and follow her to the X-ray department.

Marius and Charlie are soon back in our room. After a small family supper, I watch Marius climb on the chair and then up onto the bed. He points to the book's illustrations and shouts out the colors and words. He is a perfectly healthy and normal child. "Charlie, do you trust me?"

The light from the window begins to fade, and the shadows start to fill the room. Neither of them turned on a light.

Before Charlie can answer, Dr. Mariana is silhouetted in the door. "The results are as we thought. Marius is fine. These are of another child. They were switched. The department sends its regrets."

We get up and hug Dr. Mariana. Charlie cries. The three of us cling together as survivors. The doctor is also exhausted. "I am leaving orders for an IV medication to help Marius sleep through the night. You two also get some rest." She looks over at Marius, who is now climbing up and over Charlie's shoulders. And she quietly closes the door, waving goodbye just before it shuts.

My question to Charlie hangs in the fading light. We lean on each other in the middle of the room. Marius has gone over and found a new bag of toys that have been left at our door. He busily starts pulling them out one by one.

"Yes, Flori, I trust you. I married a beautiful and intelligent woman. I trust you." Silence hangs between us. Charlie whispers, "Will you ever trust me again?"

I pause, in commitment, not doubt. "Yes, Charlie. I trust you. I have never stopped trusting you." We hold each other for several minutes. The dark room blankets us, comforting our awakening awareness of love's vulnerability.

"What we need to do is to learn to trust ourselves again," Charlie says, still wiping tears from his cheeks.

"Yes, we will need to help each other do that."

And my mind wonders, *How will this change us? Will it be possible to be normal ever again? Some things just pass away. What will pass away in light of all of this? What can stay the same?*

CHAPTER 27

Tulcea County Hospital, Tulcea, Romania
August 7, 1991, evening

FLORI SETTLED INTO THE ROOM for the first whole night. They spoke about being joyful and sad. They heard the great news that freed them from the heartache and guilt that their son had brain damage. But at the same time, another family was told their son had a skull fracture. The other family heard the dark side of the clerical switching mix-up. Some other family had to put down relief and pick up tragedy. Flori and Charlie thought of the other family's heartache.

"I am so happy. Then I think someone's son is so badly injured, and I am sad again."

"It is unfair," Charlie said, "But nothing is fair about any child's brain injury." It was comforting to speak in the dark room.

A new nurse came into the room with the prescription Dr. Mariana had written for Marius in his chart. She was a pleasant woman who usually worked on a different floor that specialized with adults. The two mothers chatted about young children and sleeping habits. Common ground, easy conversation. She turned on a small light on the wooden table next to the crib.

Flori was surprised about the size of the syringe. "That seems so much larger than the other prescriptions."

"Yes, well, it goes into the IV tube, not into his arm."

"He tried to pull the IV out all last night. I think that is what kept me awake, checking on him."

"Well, we want you both to sleep tonight. I can reposition the IV into his head, and remove it from his arm. Would that be worth a try?"

"Sure, that might work." Flori watched as the nurse expertly repositioned the IV and taped it carefully to Marius's head.

"Good night." And the nurse was gone.

Flori and Charlie sang Marius a song, stroking his forehead and kissing his fingers. Very quickly he was sound asleep. They were exhausted but not sleepy. The clock loudly ticked off the minutes.

Flori buttoned and unbuttoned the sweater Aunt Cristina had brought. It was so quiet. And then suddenly, it was unbearably quiet and still. "Charlie!" Flori looked over at her husband, and worry and anxiety were evident in her eyes. "I don't know. Something seems wrong. He is so sound asleep."

"Flori, enough!" Charlie stood up firmly and walked over. "You had a time today when you were worrying too much. You are not going to go back to that again. Are you?"

"He seems to be sleeping too deeply."

Charlie rolled his eyes. Then he stopped, took a deep breath, and put his arm around her shoulders.

"Look, the doctor wanted him to sleep. She prescribed medicine to help him sleep. He is sleeping, and now you are worrying something is wrong." There was a more patient tone to Charlie's comment.

But the very question was upsetting to Flori. Considering what has happened, hasn't she handled it better than anyone could expect a mother to handle such trials? She wondered how the other child's mother was handling the recent bad news. She looked up at him. She was too tired to discuss this. Like Charlie's announcement this morning, it was time to let some things pass and deal with them later if necessary. She backed away from Charlie and leaned against the wall and closed her eyes.

Within minutes, her eyes snapped open and immediately focused on the IV bag hanging above Marius's head. It was empty and flat. The sedative had flowed much faster than Flori expected. Marius had rolled over and was now sleeping on the bag's plastic tube. She tried to turn Marius over into a better position. Marius was heavy, very heavy. His arms and legs seemed disconnected from his body, limp and non-responsive to her attempts to turn him. None of the endearing movements of the night before reassured her anxiety. She tried to disrupt his comfort by tickling his foot. He did not pull his foot back, and she touched him again. This time he did, ever so slightly. Marius was breathing, but it seemed different compared to his breathing the night before. Flori took the chart and opened it. She looked at Marius. Charlie was trying to have him stir or awaken him a bit to ease her anxiety.

He looked up at her. "He is very limp."

"Look here at the chart. It says 1 ml, but the syringe says 10.0 ml. That is ten times more. I think 10.0 ml is the adult dosage. See how the doctor wrote, and this could look like an extra zero."

The whole bag had emptied into Marius's vein—ten times the amount that should have been administered. Charlie raced down the hall and called for help. Doctor Mariana was leaning against the nurses' station making a notation in a patient chart. She had completed double shifts the day before, and she still had not gone home.

Charlie shouted, "Marius got 10 ml!"

"What? This cannot be!" Her eyes widened, and she dropped the chart onto the desk. "No, 1 ml!" She ran down the hall, passing Charlie. Marius's nurse also came around the corner and saw Dr. Mariana running toward the baby's room. "What is wrong?"

Quickly another younger nurse from behind the counter explained. They both ran past Charlie toward the room.

"Let me see the chart!" Dr. Mariana charged into the room and grabbed it from Flori. "It says 1.0 ml. That is right."

Flori said, "The nurse put the whole 10.0 ml dose into the IV bag, and it has all flowed into Marius. She gave him ten times the correct dosage!"

"What? No!" The doctor removed the IV bag from the stand just as the nurses arrived at the door. She looked at the nurse and shouted, "1.0 ml! One! Not 10 ml!"

Marius's nurse became whiter than her uniform. "I gave him what is written. 10.0 ml." She picked up the chart from the bed where the doctor had dropped it. She pointed to the chart. "See 10.0 ml!"

Doctor Mariana ignored the nurse as she was assessing Marius's heartbeat and breathing. She also tested his reactions, which seemed delayed and weak. She grabbed the chart away from the nurse. But the nurse leaned over and pointed to the writing. "See. 10 ml!"

"No, it is 1.0 ml!"

They were both silent, as the misunderstanding became apparent to each. The nurse lowered her voice and shook her head slowly. "It looks like 10.0 ml to me."

Doctor Mariana turned her back to the nurse and faced Charlie and Flori. "Okay, I will start another IV and flush out the sedative all night. I will stay and monitor him. I will take care of him."

Other nurses came in, and plans were made to keep him in clean diapers, check his urine and blood frequently, and keep a bedside check for his breathing and pulse through the night.

Charlie and Flori stepped back against the wall nearest to their son to allow the staff to work. The desperate action to reduce the effects of the sedative reinforced the seriousness of the situation. How could there be one more thing threatening their son?

"We will have to wait and see if there is damage from this. I do not think there will be lasting effects, but we will need to wait and see how the night goes." Dr. Mariana's face showed the stress of her ordeal also. "I understand your fear. Here is a note to allow you as much access to Marius as you want."

The medical staff continued to work on Marius's care. Finally, Dr. Mariana and another doctor asked the Madas to come out into the hallway. "Marius is stable. He does not need oxygen now. His blood shows he is getting enough on his own. Although he is not in a coma, we think he will sleep for most of three-and-a-half days. This is not related to any injury. As long as we watch him very closely, he will recover completely."

There was a lot Flori and Charlie might have thought and said at this moment. But angry words were not going to heal their son. Words were not going to eliminate their fears. They had no place to turn. They had no other place to go to make this better. It was going to be what it was going to be. The doctors left, and nurses seemed to take over the supervision. Charlie and Flori stood in the doorway.

Flori said, "Charlie, I am so afraid. What else will happen?" She broke down in tears. "There cannot be brain damage now. I want Marius."

Charlie held her against his chest. He could not look into her eyes. She would see how afraid he felt too. Several moments passed, and he wondered what he could say to comfort his wife. How could he be strong enough? But then Charlie saw all the people rushing into the room, not to harm Marius, but to help him. "He will be okay. He will live. We did not come this far to lose him. Dr. Mariana said he is breathing without any help. He has a steady pulse. His heartbeat is strong. He is going to make it."

Flori didn't say anything, but Charlie could feel strength come back into her legs, and she stood a bit taller. He was in no rush to move. There was nothing they could do. One more time they chose to put down the anger and tension, and instead, they chose to treasure these moments with their son.

And so, throughout the night, they watched their son sleep. Marius was somewhere else, in some deep untouchable place. But his mother and father stood guard over their son to prevent even their doubts from surging up, breaking out, and taking over.

"It will be okay, Marius. We will take you to your favorite parks and let you swing and climb until you want to go home." Charlie winked at Flori. She couldn't help smiling back.

"You will be like other children," Flori whispered. "No! No! You will be better than other children, or at least we will always think so."

Charlie put his arm around Flori and squeezed. "No, he will be very smart and good-looking too." Charlie put his hands over his eyes and trembled. Even their positive thoughts and desires evoked tears. The war between hope and despair raged around them. They touched Marius's forehead and held his hands. Flori read and inspected the label of every bag hung on the IV pole, and she talked to every nurse who took his pulse or listened to his heartbeat.

But mostly, they talked to Marius and to themselves. "You are okay? We are here together. It will be better." Flori touched her son's little head, and her fingers traced his cheek. And occasionally one of them whispered, "I am sorry. You will get better and run around chasing white ducks again."

Time offered no refuge from the accumulation of grief and fear. There was just a never-ending "now." Even thinking about yesterday, today, or tomorrow was too difficult. Wearily, Flori rested her head in her hands. They had been happy at the exact moment Marius had fallen into the pipe. If even during the best moments, life was this fragile, how could any moment ever feel normal again? She shuddered at the decision that seemed so clear. *Darkness or light?* She could choose to look into that abyss every day, apparently every second. Or she could choose not to see it at all.

"Charlie, we must only think of Marius getting better. Nothing else. Just that."

"Okay, Flori, that is what I want to do also." But he also felt it was exhausting work to push so much fear away constantly.

Who would imagine this vacation had started just two days ago with such joyful abandonment of daily routines? That first night in the resort, they had fallen asleep believing a memorable vacation would follow. And the next golden morning with Marius had only helped to confirm the magic they expected. The vacation had been symbolically a celebration of Charlie and Flori's financial security, the result of insight, hard work, and wise investment. But it all seemed ridiculous now.

Charlie sat with his elbows resting on his knees and his head in his hands. He could agree with Flori to think just positive thoughts, but he could not stop the pain that fear had planted deep in his gut. He slowly moved across the room and sank into the second bed. He covered his face with his hands.

Each time Flori awoke during the night, she realized she could not choose her dreams. She was forced to relive the unbelievable events that had created their new world. She shuddered with sobs and paced between the most uncomfortable chair in the world to the side of the youth bed where their son lay motionless. She did not say anything to her husband, although she suspected he was not asleep.

Charlie silently watched her. She finally slipped into the second bed, and she had seemingly fallen asleep. But he could feel it shake with her silent cry. What was there for him to say to Flori? He tucked the covers up and over her shoulders.

CHAPTER 28

Tulcea County Hospital, Tulcea, Romania
August 8, 1991, morning

THE SHADOWS OF THE LEAVES filled the room with dancing little shadows again for just fifteen minutes, and then they were gone. Flori was asleep, her face twisted by painful dreams. Charlie liked standing at the window and looking at the huge trunk of the tree outside. It was in constant movement. It also creaked and groaned softly, and the movement of the leaves also created a sound Charlie never remembered hearing before. He thought, *All the trees are constantly moving and groaning. I do not hear that sound on busy days. But it is true. This tree will stand outside this window gently swaying, and patients and families will come and go. And this soft cracking and groaning of branches will continue. Things will change, and things will stay the same. I need to remember to listen to other trees when I am no longer here.*

Charlie went back to the apartment at nine in the morning, where he tried to eat and sleep. Within hours, he returned to the hospital. He encouraged Flori to do the same. They took turns retreating to Aunt Cristina's apartment to wash in an attempt not to show how devastated they felt on the inside. Each morning for the next two days, Charlie considered the tree a bit of an emotional escape— escape from watching Marius's unnaturally deep sleep continue. His limp, little body seldom moved. His color was good. The blood and urine tests were normal. The doctors were confident he would wake in two days.

Flori noticed there were fewer visitors to see her "miracle baby." The doctors who came in were slow to make eye contact and were less talkative. Marius's complete stillness and uninterrupted sleep created a profound sadness. Being tossed in waves of joy, confusion, and despair had exhausted Marius's parents. How could they not miss the active and adorable son who had been returned to them for a few short hours? Their son had died, and then he was returned to life. Three times, relief and joy had been snatched away from them—first with fears of the pipe, then brain injury, and now an overdose. And yet they sat at his bedside, holding on to his recovery.

Thoughts of daily routines, or plans, or past events held no interest for Flori. Their conversations faded. Charlie tried to survive in small increments of time, from sunrise to the leaf dance, to breakfast being delivered, to the doctors' visits.

CHAPTER 29

Tulcea County Hospital, Tulcea, Romania
August 10, 1991
Flori

ON THE THIRD MORNING, MARIUS'S legs begin to move under the sheets, and he even kicks them off. He moves his body when the nurses check his diaper, and his hands fuss with the IV. His eyes do not open, but as he stirs, so does my hope.

"I think he will continue to wake up today," Dr. Mariana says as she writes these observations on his chart. "It is as I had thought. His tests are all normal." She squeezes my arm confidently.

Marius drifts in and out of sleep for several hours, and each time he wakes up, we are there to whisper our welcomes and love. Soon Marius wants to be held, to curl up and feel the strength of his mama and papa's arms and the warmth of our heartbeats. I want nothing else. I relax in such bliss.

I close my eyes and feel Marius's warmth and breath, and whisper, "Can there be more relief and contentment anywhere on Earth? I will soon take you home and tuck you into your own bed, in your own home. Our lives will continue as we know them."

The three of us snuggle together and sleep in each other's arms. We find rest and sanctuary, and it is more than enough.

CHAPTER 30

Tulcea County Hospital
Tulcea, Romania
August 10, 1991
Charlie

I HOLD MY SON CAREFULLY, and I whisper in his ear, "Now, Marius, you are here with us. I love you. We can live together and be a happy family. But where, beyond Romania, am I to go?"

CHAPTER 31

Tulcea County Hospital, Tulcea, Romania
August 10, 1991

BY LUNCH, MARIUS BECAME MORE alert and active. He wiggled down
off one of their laps and wobbled over to the other parent and then
back again. He held onto the bed and cautiously took a few steps.
He was quiet, but he asked for a cup of water. Flori began to worry
things were not right. Was Marius slurring his speech? Was it gar-
bled? Flori usually could understand Marius's speech, but she too had
to guess at what he was saying.

"Does he have brain damage now?"

Charlie tried to remember whether during the brief time before
waking and the overdose Marius had the same trouble. Had he used
the same words then? "I don't know. I don't know."

After lunch, Marius started walking across the room, and it was
clear he was struggling. He was wobbling more because one side was
not responding and dragging a bit behind. Flori's heart dropped.
Mountains of fear appeared, and she didn't have the strength to
climb them. On the horizon, other distant mountain ranges loomed.
An endless number of obstacles and complications seemed possible.
When would they know all of the effects of this overdose?

Unexpectedly, nurses informed them they were going to move
Marius from the single room to a room on the children's ward. Flori's
first reaction was that Marius wasn't ready to leave this single room.
She wasn't ready. Since the expected fevers and infectious complications had not developed, the IV had been removed. The nurses

explained the coordination difficulties and slurred speech did not require a private room, so they could continue to monitor his progress and meet his needs in a pediatric ward. Soon the Madas were packed up and moved into a room with three other children. There were two beds along each wall with a window at the far end. All three of the children were sleeping, so the mothers waved a silent welcome.

CHAPTER 32

Tulcea County Hospital, Tulcea, Romania
August 11, 1991

MARIUS SLEPT ALL NIGHT PEACEFULLY. So very early the next morning, Flori left him in Charlie's care and went back to the apartment for a few hours of sleep. Then she showered, styled her hair, and ate. She had her bags from the hotel, and Aunt Cristina had cleaned and pressed her better clothes. Flori found her makeup and enjoyed applying her red lipstick. She tucked her blouse into her slim skirt and slipped on three-inch white heels. Looking in the mirror, she was surprised she looked like the same person. Because so much had happened, she didn't think she could look the same. Nevertheless, a shower and lipstick had offered temporary magic that revived Flori. She could feel new energy when she walked down the long hallway.

"I could hear your footsteps in the hall, and I recognized your walk," Charlie smiled. He liked her heels, and she enjoyed his admiration. He explained although Marius had enjoyed a peaceful night's sleep, the early morning noises and cramped chair had not been comfortable for him.

"Go home. I feel a thousand times better after sleeping, showering, and eating!" Flori insisted, and Charlie agreed.

Marius also seemed revived. He was not going to stay in his bed. Flori gave him her full attention. She read his books, and they played with stuffed toys. They would hide the little dog and then try to find it under the pillow,

"Is Toy Dog here?"

"No!"

"Around the folds of the sheet?"

"No!"

"Under the blanket?"

"Yes!" And then they played it all over again.

Soon, however, Marius wanted to get down and play with the other children. When they didn't respond, he began to pull off the blankets from one of the beds. "I think he is trying to look for the stuffed dog. He wants to play," Flori explained. He asked the other mothers hundreds of questions, and it was clear he was annoying them. Suddenly, Flori realized his speech was clear and his walking steady! Tears flowed! She couldn't stop. His coordination, his speech, and his charm were all perfectly Marius. He was himself!

Flori's tears washed away layers and layers of tension. She needed a dozen tissues to keep her makeup from following her tears down her cheeks. Although she tried to restrain Marius's insistent attention to the other children, she was enthralled watching his normal behavior. He was acting as though he was reaching out to other children in the park's playground. How could she tell him, "No", or, "Stop?"

The other mothers watched her and understood something profound was happening. They had heard this was "the miracle baby." He had seemed so healthy; they could not understand the miracle. But watching Flori react to him helped them see there was more to the story than they had known.

By mid-afternoon, Charlie returned, and Flori and he enjoyed observing all the ways Marius had returned to normal.

"Charlie, it is now almost impossible for me to discipline Marius!" Flori laughed.

Charlie winked at her. "I cannot either. It is true. I am not sure I will ever think he has done something wrong!"

Marius was a bit too demanding in approaching the other children, who were not as well as he was and couldn't play as he wanted. The nurses kept shooing him back to his bed and smiling, because it was clear he was very healthy.

"Okay, Marius," Flori said in her best stern voice. "You must be a good boy to be back to your old self. You were the best, little boy. Come and sit on my lap and read more books. Maybe Daddy will bring you some of your favorite toys."

Charlie reassured them he would pick some up during his next trip to Aunt Cristina's apartment. "I want to get Dr. Mariana a gift. I want to get her a huge bouquet of flowers," Charlie added, "and one for the supervisor doctor too."

Flori thought it was a great idea, and Charlie quickly found a small shop the nurses had explained was fairly close to the hospital. It was a small showroom, and there were not many flowers displayed in the coolers.

"I want to buy two very large arrangements of flowers," Charlie told the shop lady behind the counter.

"Oh, yes. But it is August. It is too hot for local flowers. I must order them. If I can get them, it will be several days."

Charlie was shocked. He had expected to walk out with two armfuls of beautiful flowers.

"What about those?" He pointed to several buckets in the back-room filled with flowers.

"Oh, those are for a funeral. Someone has bought them already."

"Oh no. I need flowers for a lady doctor who saved my child's life!"

The shop woman looked up from her pad. "Really? Was it a boy? Was it your little boy?" she asked.

Charlie was taken aback. "Yes. He drowned, and now he is alive! I wanted to present her with flowers."

The flower lady smiled and exclaimed, "The miracle boy?"

"How do you know my son's story?" Charlie asked.

"Everyone knows. Everyone in town is talking about it. The Promenade is better than our newspaper. So many people have heard this story from their friends who were in the hospital or work there. It is the favorite story out there."

Charlie broke out into a smile and laughed. His "miracle boy" was not just their excitement, but he was the joy of the city. He felt like he was being lifted by shared elation.

"Yes, it is a miracle. The doctor said he was dead, and now he is alive. She declared he was a miracle. And now he seems normal. It is like nothing ever happened."

The woman came out from behind the counter and hugged Charlie. "I will find you flowers. I will use some from the funeral order, and I will find others. Come back before I close. I will have your bouquets."

Charlie returned to wait at the hospital, and he found Flori and Marius had made progress making friends with the other children. One patient was a younger little girl who kept calling Flori her Mommy.

Marius did not like sharing his mommy. He shouted to the girl to stop, and the younger girl began to cry. Flori had once again gathered Marius into her arms and brought him back to their area of the room. She wrapped her arms around him, controlling his anger and behavior.

"Relax, Marius. I am here. See how much we love you. Aren't you happy that you are here now with your mommy and daddy?"

Marius stopped and looked intently at Flori. He pulled back and slapped her face. The force surprised Flori, and her knees buckled. Marius's sudden and extreme change in attitude left her confused and shaken. Immediately, Marius began to scream, an inconsolable scream that came with a torrent of tears. Just as suddenly, he wrapped his arms around her and held on with a desperate urgency. In spite of her attention and comfort, she could not calm Marius from the anguish or the anger that had overtaken him. Big tears flowed freely from his eyes, onto his nose, and down his cheeks. His nose turned red and his cheeks scarlet. It was not an emotional reaction either parent had ever seen before. It was over twenty minutes before Marius was able to calm down with exhaustion. Flori had used all her strength to hold Marius during this time.

But it was her soul that ached. She knew something had happened. Was Marius overcome with memories and emotions from falling into the pipe? By being alone in the dark, damp pipe? Had he called for her? She was terrified for her son. How could she help him heal from such an experience? For although every tiny detail of the tragic accident would be burned into Charlie's and her memories, Marius had been alone in his experience. The darkness of the pipe and her child feeling trapped and abandoned was a new terror. How could she expect them to have the same relationship? Would Marius always be haunted by some shadow of memory that she had failed to care for him? Had his parents not been enough? Would this rage be knit into his personality? Finally, he fell asleep, and this nap had come as a blessing for everyone in the room.

The nurses and other parents had been unnerved by his outburst. "What did you say to him?" one mother asked once he was asleep. "He went from fine to terrified in a second."

"I don't know why. My baby never hit me before. I only asked him if he was happy."

The other mother looked skeptical. Flori wished they were back in the private room. She was embarrassed her baby had hit her so hard. She was confused by his terrified, angry outburst, and she did not know what she should do if it happened again.

By late afternoon, Charlie had picked up the bouquets. Just as Charlie had heard her steps in the hall that morning, Flori recognized his quick and happy step. She went to the door and smiled. There was her tall husband, dressed and handsome, and carrying a huge, beautiful bouquet of flowers. The enormous collection of flowers was more beautiful than any Flori had ever seen. An equally elegant bow was tied around the stems. People stopped and smiled when he passed, as both Charlie and the flowers were impressive.

"They are amazing, Charlie."

"Yes, when the lady brought them out, I couldn't believe it. She said she'd rather send them to express gratitude for the living than the dead. Funeral flowers turned to 'thankyou' flowers." Charlie had a smile as big as Flori had ever seen. "They include something called sea holly, and see this violet daisy? Even the lady at the shop was surprised she could get these in the dry season. They are spring flowers. I am so proud to be able to take them to Doctor Mariana. Supervisor Helena was also thrilled when I left them with her."

"Charlie, you did a great job."

He went off to present them to Doctor Mariana. When he walked around the corner, Doctor Mariana started to cry. Later, Charlie sheepishly told Flori he had also broken down. They had said little. "It was all I could do to say thank you and keep standing. But everyone around her said how beautiful they were. The flowers honored her as we wished. But she is modest. She said she did nothing, that only God could do such a miracle. She again told me to thank God, only him."

CHAPTER 33

Tulcea, Romania
August 12, 1991

THE NEXT MORNING DID BRING new drama. Thankfully not drama centered on Marius. To the extreme north, flooding had resulted in great damage to the land and many residences, resulting in injured and homeless citizens. The disruption to the communities had created public health dangers. Increasing numbers of people were coming down with high fevers and intestinal infections. The hospitals nearer the affected areas were at capacity, and patients were beginning to be transferred to Tulcea County Hospital.

"I don't want your child to be exposed to diseases that might be admitted with foreign patients. We need to clear the hospital of those who are not receiving active nursing and treatment. Incredible as it is, Marius is my healthiest patient. I do not want you to leave the city for at least another four days. Could you stay with your aunt and bring Marius to my office at 8:00 a.m. each day? You will enter a specific door, and I will prepare a special room. No sick patients will be present or use that door or room. I do not want you in a hotel. You may only stay in a private home. Can you do that?"

"Yes, my aunt will let us stay with her." The three of them joked about taking advantage of kind relatives. But Flori and Charlie were happy to look forward to more private and comfortable surroundings. The four-family room had been challenging.

"Wonderful. Marius is officially registered as an ambulatory patient. I will see you tomorrow morning."

Within an hour, Charlie and Flori were knocking on Aunt Cristina's door. It was a huge surprise for her to see Marius. It was the sweetest of homecomings. Aunt Cristina couldn't have made them feel more welcome in her home.

Flori caught her looking at the little boy. "Oh, Flori, oh, Flori," is all her aunt said.

CHAPTER 34

Tulcea, Romania
August 15, 1991
Flori

THE EARLY MORNING VISITS TO Dr. Mariana are quick and efficient. It doesn't take long because Marius is the picture of health. He is showing off by charming everyone with his smile and funny comments. "You are tall," he tells Lady Mariana, reaching with his hand far above his head and then jumping.

"Yes, I am!" she laughs. "And you are very special although you are not tall."

Later in the afternoon, I suggest, "Let's take a walk when he wakes up from his nap and find a church. We promised Dr. Lady Mariana we would, and today is August 15th, the Feast of Saint Maria."

Charlie smiles at the irony, nods in agreement, and replies, "You are not worried about diseases?"

"No, we will not let anyone hold him. He will be in the stroller, and we will be outside."

"Okay, let's go!" Charlie beams at my confidence.

"We will start on the Promenade, and if we do not see a church, we can ask directions."

Within hours, we step out on the Promenade. It is close to the entrance to Aunt Cristina's apartment. The Promenade is a lovely, broad, walking path along the Danube River. It is lined on the right side with apartment buildings like Cristina's, enjoying expansive views of the Danube Preserve. The afternoon could not be lovelier with seventy-five degrees Fahrenheit and a slight breeze, and it is not too crowded.

People dress elegantly. Men wear suits and ties, and their shoes are polished daily. They look successful enough to have time to relax. Women also wear expensive skirts and blouses. Their bags are excellent leather, and their hair is fashionably styled. They take the time to reapply flawless makeup before taking a late afternoon stroll. Like our walks in the park at home, it is the place to greet friends and business contacts, and it is a time to make new ones. Appearances convey confidence, and nurturing contacts has been very important in Communist Romania.

Charlie mentions how others hold their heads and walk with confident postures. I stand on my toes even though I am wearing three-inch heels. He laughs and stands a little taller. We don't know anyone, but we walk proudly. We are an obviously happy, young couple with an adorable baby son. People smile and greet us. Older ladies carrying large, round loaves of rich, dark, Romanian bread in their net bags wave and smile at the baby from behind their colorful scarves. The cultural custom continues here on the Promenade.

As we turn onto the pedestrian-only area, the river takes a wide bend, showing off the natural beauty of the wilderness preserve on the opposite shore. White and blue tourist boats are tied to pilings and each other, creating floating docks. The boats are enclosed on the lower levels and open on the second stories with only colorful canvas roofs. Iron railings surround the decks filled with wooden benches. With Tulcea's busy city streets behind us, we enjoy the unique character of the riverbank and an afternoon treat at fine sidewalk cafe.

We are in no hurry to find a church. We are enjoying the stroll along the Promenade all the way until the river makes a little turn inland. Here we merge onto a lovely street, Strada Unirii, which we follow through a pleasant, residential neighborhood. I point out several ornate spires topped with Orthodox crosses above the rooftops of the homes. But we continue to wander. Why would we be in a hurry? It is a lovely neighborhood with family homes and tall trees lining the streets. Watching normal family activities is a welcome relief for our overloaded emotions. We are enjoying ourselves.

"What will we do there?" Charlie asks. "I am not sure what we are going to do."

"Charlie, we will watch and see what everyone else is doing. We will do the same." I smile because I am not sure what others will be doing. "Maybe we will light candles. When I was young my grandmother took me to church, and we lit a candle for the living. On another wall, there were candles for the dead. So we will see." I shrug and smile at my husband.

"Okay, let's go. We will find a special church, and we will thank God. We have promised Dr. Lady Mariana." To prove his point, Charlie asks directions to the nearest church.

"Turn right at the next corner of Strada Babadag. There is an important church in that neighborhood. Keep going up the hill. You will see it." The man doesn't stop walking, finishing explaining the directions by looking over his shoulder.

"Okay, next right. I think!" Charlie smiles down at me. "Light candles, kiss the icons. No problem. In and out."

St. Nicholas Church, the Cathedral of Tulcea, was built on a triangle of land formed by three streets. The stone and brick church building was built in 1865, with three towers over eighty feet high in the Byzantine style of architecture. Impressive stairs cascade down in front like a waterfall.

"Lovely, Charlie. We found a beautiful church!" I am pleased by the impressive church. Suddenly, I recognize the walk of a tall woman who is exiting the middle of the three two-story-high, arched doors. She is hurrying down the steps. "Charlie, isn't that …"

But Charlie has seen her too and is already calling out, "Doctor Mariana! Doctor Mariana!"

The doctor immediately stops and turns toward us. She looks shocked. "Hello! What are you doing here?"

I laugh. "We told you we would go to church and thank God."

Charlie adds, "We promised you we would, and we are here to thank him."

"Yes, but I thought you only said that to please me. I saw your faces. But you did good, because God gave Marius to you for a second time." She leans down and touches Marius's rosy cheek. He smiles back at her. "Oh, you are mine to remember, Marius! You are my special one." She looks up and says to us, "But how or why are you here at this church?"

"We didn't know you would be here, Doctor. We were just walking and thought we would find one of the churches we were told was near. To start we only had vague directions, but here we are. And then we saw you!"

"And you just happened to arrive here, just as I was leaving?" The doctor looks up toward the sky or steeple, and she smiles. "It is so good you came, and that I saw you and know you came. Well, it pleases me to see you here. I am due back at the hospital, and we will see each other tomorrow." We exchange friendly waves, and she rushes off.

I hold Charlie's hand as we watch her hurry down the stairs and cross the street. "What good fortune to see Dr. Mariana here," Charlie sighs.

"Yes, it is a sign. It is good we are here thanking God, and it is very good to be here at Saint Nicolas Church of Tulcea!"

Inside the church are two walls of candles, just as I remember from my grandmother's church—one for the living and one for the dead. I very carefully light a candle for the living, whispering, "Marius, for Marius. God, thank you."

As Charlie leaves a generous donation in the metal box, I look at all the candles flickering in the dark church. Do each represent a miracle? Our miracle is so great that even the Dr. Lady Mariana comes to light candles of gratitude. And yet, here are over one hundred candles, each for a mother or father or son or daughter. Each represents a prayer for living in this dangerous and difficult world. It seems surprising that Marius's candle does not burn any brighter than the others. I just look at them all, and I don't know what to think of so many mysteries.

Tourists are listening to a tour guide. We hear about the beautiful and historically valuable paintings in the Renaissance style by a

Romanian artist in 1905 that cover the walls of the sanctuary. The murals and icons, in gold and red and translucent blue paints, are some of the richest we have ever seen, even in this Russian Orthodox country. Traditional Orthodox congregations respect Iconic portraits, ascribing to them miracles and a deepening of faith.

In the back of the church, an old man is busy painting a copy of one. We watch the slow, intricate way his tiny brush of squirrel hair hardly touches the surface. He creates something of such great beauty, slowly and with prayer. With the other tourists, we kiss the most important icon, make another donation, and walk back toward the three large church doors.

Charlie squeezes my hand, "We have come to an impressive church to light just one small candle. Meeting Dr. Mariana only confirms we have done the right thing to find this church and thank God this lovely, summer afternoon." Just before we walk out into the glaring light beyond the doors, I look back. Somewhere, a quiet chant is echoing high in the rafters of the church, bouncing among tall, rounded windows. Strong incense burns to lift the faithful prayers to heaven, and below, the candles create a soft, gentle light, a flickering expression of the mystery of God's mercy.

As we leave the church, I look up at the three spires reaching into the sky and think, *This will always be an important church to me. This is our moment and our church. This is part of our story.*

CHAPTER 35

Tulcea, Romania
August 16, 1991

FLORI AND CHARLIE RETURNED FROM the last appointment with Dr. Mariana and shared the good news with Aunt Cristina. "Yes, Marius has been officially released from the hospital and permitted to return to Bucharest in two days. All we were told to do was to report to Marius's baby doctor and to present the basic medical documents."

Everyone was both excited and surprised by such great progress. Aunt Cristina offered to read Marius a story. Flori took the medical documents out to read. She was surprised that the medical records stated that Marius came to the hospital in a Stage Four Coma, brain dead, inconsistent with any hope of recovery. The hospital did not admit patients if there were no measurable signs of life. Doctor Lady Mariana's decision to place Marius in a bed and allow his parents to be at his bedside was against hospital policy. Even the district supervisor had agreed on the unusual plan, so the doctors could keep an eye on the Madas and help them accept his death. Doctor Lady Mariana said they were all worried that one or both of them would have a breakdown.

All the records began with the moment the medical staff could treat Marius, at the moment when Dr. Mariana had seen that he was no longer dead, but alive. Flori and Charlie accepted it. They had no reason to want more, as the entire staff had been very forthcoming verbally that they had not seen any living signs for over seven hours. But when they could treat a living child, they had done so.

The mistakes in the administration of the sedative were also in the reports, without explanation. Flori and Charlie were ready to move on, and they were not interested in an investigation that would cause Dr. Mariana or anyone else any troubles. Free medical care included unquestioned care. They had left deeply satisfied with the outcome.

As they began planning the trip home, they wondered how the family would react to the news of the accident. It all unfolded so quickly. It was too confusing to begin to find the words to explain. Flori didn't look forward to explaining how Marius fell undetected into a pipe, nor did she want to find the words that would express the terror and pain of that day.

CHAPTER 36

Tulcea and Ukraine
Ferry Trip to Ismail, Ukraine
August 16–17, 1991
Flori

AUNT CRISTINA HUGS ME AND suggests to Charlie a plan. "You need to be together. You need to talk and to share and have some time to help each other get through this troubled week. Go. Go. I will watch Marius tomorrow. I will stay in the apartment and just look at only him. You two take a ferry and go across the Danube River into Ukraine. You came here for a vacation. Take a day for yourselves before you return home."

The night before, Aunt Cristina and I had decided she would make this suggestion. I had confided in her that Charlie was still insisting he had to leave Romania. Distraught and confused, I was still in shock he would suggest this even once, but he had brought up the subject perhaps four times in the last few days!

"He is uncertain when or how to leave and where to go. And that doesn't seem to upset him in the least. He says he is as certain of his need to leave Romania as I was certain Marius would live. He doesn't understand it, but he believes it. He only says he must leave."

Aunt Cristina is known in our family for giving wise advice. She has seen Marius without breath, and she understands the miracle as well as anyone else. She also has seen what we have gone through in the last week. It was easy to turn to her to discuss my growing anxiety about Charlie.

I explain, "I would think it was a nervous breakdown, without any nervousness. He is just showing an unnatural and infuriating calmness and contentment. Is that possible? I know it seems crazy, but what hasn't been crazy? He doesn't seem the least bit concerned with the details or complications with the business or our family. He is calm, alarmingly calm, and happy."

"Well, what does he exactly mean by saying he needs to leave Romania? To go where?"

I look at Cristina and say, "I don't know, and I don't think he knows. Unlike the way Charlie usually is, he is not worried or anxious about not knowing details or plans."

"Perhaps if you go with him just across the Danube to Izmail, Ukraine, he will relax and feel he has left Romania. He might just feel he did what he was supposed to do—leave Romania, and then he can move on. You will go back to Bucharest, and the trauma and stress of this accident and experience will begin to fade," suggests Cristina.

"Aunt Cristina, I have not told you something. Charlie says he needs to leave Romania, not we need to leave Romania. I am afraid to ask if he intends to leave without me. To leave us," I cry. It is exhausting fending off such confusing emotions.

After an evening considering her plan, I decide it is worth a try. Against all of my motherly instincts never to leave Marius's side again, and much to Charlie's pleasant surprise, I accept Aunt Cristina's plan. After putting Marius down for an afternoon's nap, Charlie and I take our passports to the travel agency and buy tickets for the next morning's tour.

On August 17, 1991, we board a ferry to Izmail, Ukraine. The ferry moves slowly; most of the passengers are tourists on a day trip. The skies are a bit gray in the early morning, casting a silver silence across the marshes. The Danube River flows from the German Black Forest to the Black Sea. The ferry crosses the river just before the river splits into three separate rivers that meander through the marsh, reeds, and grass floodplains. The three rivers create a very large delta as they slow and spill into the sea. Because this highly unique wilderness environment is the home to numerous rare species of plants and animals, guides help vacationers spot a rare bird or see an unusual flower. There are explanations how the Danube has such abundant sources of groundwater that over twenty-three separate ecosystems can thrive. It is a wonderfully unique place.

"It is beautiful and peaceful," I begin.

"Yes, it is. It is hard to understand no matter what we are going through on any given day, the river flows just like this."

We lean against the railing to stare into the distance. I wonder if we are looking at our past or our future. It is now impossible to anticipate my husband's thoughts. Aunt Cristina's advice was, "Don't talk much. Just listen to him, especially when he isn't talking."

So I study the strong features of his face. He seems unexplainably relaxed and happy. He looks over and catches me looking at him. "You are quiet, Flori. Are you enjoying yourself?"

"Yes, I am happy to be here with you."

And here we stand on the deck of the ferry trying to take deep breaths of the sea air. The recent week has been a roller coaster of difficult and frightening events. Now we are on a boat surrounded by people who are unaware of our trials. For the fellow passengers, it is a relaxing voyage, but we are trying to piece together a huge jigsaw puzzle. There are pieces with familiar shapes and colors that we can quickly piece together.

"I was so scared," I whisper.

"Flori, I was so scared too. I have never felt anything like that. I was afraid I would fail him. That I would fail you."

And then we share all that we still don't understand.

"How did you know Marius was in the pipe before we saw him? I do not know how you were so sure."

"I do not know how I knew that. There was something in my chest insisting I knew it. I could not ignore the knowing."

We try to relive the happy parts of such an awful story.

"Wasn't it funny when Dr. Mariana saw Marius alive?"

"Yes! When I told her that our son was alive, she did not believe it because she thought I was just talking gibberish," Charlie laughs. "Maybe I was talking gibberish. I was so excited. I could not believe it either!"

I add, "But no one was more surprised. She said he was dead, and she sees death. She had never seen someone dead become alive."

There were also times the puzzle pieces look disjointed and unfamiliar, and we make no progress. "Why did this happen to us?"

"Do you mean the bad or the good things that have happened?"

"I don't know. Both?"

Charlie says, "I have learned some things. Have you?"

"Yes," I say, "I will never be the same. But I will be all right. But if we had lost Marius, I don't think I would have ever been able to overcome the guilt. My sorrow would have destroyed me. I do not know how I could have continued to be a wife. I don't know how I could have forgiven us. People do, but I do not know how. I am not sure what would have happened."

And then we find shapes of emotions that only fit together with fear and anguish.

"I still feel so weak," Charlie mumbles to the open spaces. "I am haunted by how powerless I am. Maybe we would never have found his body or never have known what happened to our Marius. I was afraid I could not get his body out." We break down and sob. It doesn't matter others might wonder why. It just doesn't matter.

"Charlie, now I understand how quickly everything can be gone. I understand I must be more careful defining 'everything.' 'Everything' isn't the collection of many things. It can be one thing. 'Everything' sounds substantial, but it is more fragile than I expected it to be."

We find the pieces that show us how important being truthful should be. We renew our vows to be completely truthful. We agree that telling the truth is necessary, and telling the whole truth is even more necessary. We will not lie to Marius about what happened. We dedicate ourselves to raising Marius to treasure life and family before business or social success.

Painfully, we put together the pieces that show our regrets. "I want to say, 'I love you,' more. I want to say it to you all the time, Charlie. I want you to know that every morning and every night. And I want to say it to Marius. I want to fill our house with expressions of love, so that it is not just understood, but always shared." I look at him, smile, and begin to feel the tears running out my nose. Charlie laughs and hands me his handkerchief.

"Marius will just have to get used to being embarrassed by us. We are going to kiss him whenever we want to and say we love him in front of his friends. I am going to kiss his head in his sleep every night," Charlie laughs. "Even when he is a man, I will kiss him whenever I want! But we need to find a way to be good parents and discipline him when necessary!"

I laugh, "Marius is a good boy, so it won't be necessary too often." The boat's horn bellows out a few notes to a passing large ship. I wait for the quiet of the river to return. "Charlie, I am still confused and unsure of all that happened. I feel like things spun out of control, and all I have are intense emotions to remember. The days just don't seem real, as if the earth somehow moved and there is nowhere safe to stand."

As the sunset begins reflecting across the delta plain, we realize we have only started to understand this experience. We have made progress, but we are not sure we have all the puzzle pieces. And some of the pieces are so dark, we don't want to hunt for them. After this experience, what would the future look like? And without knowing, it was hard to trust in the normalcy we are experiencing now on the Danube River.

Twice we talk about Charlie's insistence he must leave Romania. "You understand how you knew Marius was in the pipe? That is how I know I must leave Romania. It is not my idea. I do not want to leave Romania. But I know I must. When I trusted you about the pipe, how did it make you feel?"

"It made me love you more. It made me feel that you loved me."

"Yes, and trusting you then was my best plan. I had others. But trusting you, when you could not give me reasons, made us stronger. If we had lost Marius, it was not because I did not trust you. I don't have a plan, but when it unfolds, we need to be bold, and without fear, go forward. I need you to trust me in the same way. If it doesn't work out, it won't be because you did not trust me. It will make us stronger, even if we never understand."

Our adjustments are not over as the boat comes in sight of its dock back in Romania. I think we will take out the emotional puzzle pieces from this day. Little, life-pieces will continue to come together and clarify our portrait. I begin to understand that the image can be beautiful, even when it isn't perfect or complete.

Charlie smiles and pulls me closer. I close my eyes and think, *Don't leave us, Charlie.* I bury my face in his shirt, and he kisses my head.

"I love you, Flori. From the bus stop, I have loved you."

CHAPTER 37

Bucharest, Romania
April 18, 1982 to 1991
Meeting and Marrying

CHARLIE AND FLORI FIRST MET when she was waiting at a bus stop
for a ride home from the city. She and Elena, a friend and co-worker
at the factory, had enjoyed spending the day at Herastrau Park. It
was a lovely April Easter Day, and families and friends gathered
in the park to enjoy the floral displays and eat holiday food from
vendors. Charlie and his cousin, whom Flori had briefly dated,
rode by the bus stop. Charlie looked at the lively, beautiful girl
and slowed down. She had recognized Charlie and his cousin and
waved hello.

Charlie immediately offered the girls a ride, and Flori accepted.
He was tall, good-looking, and he was a driving instructor with a car.
He had always made a good impression, with entertaining stories
and a casual confidence. Perhaps they would hit it off and date, but
if they just became friends, she might still convince him to give her
driving lessons.

The offer to take them directly to Flori's house and avoid the
bus ride was irresistible. The girls agreed, and Flori climbed into the
front seat next to Charlie. Her pale complexion was surrounded by
soft waves of curls that blew in the wind from the open windows.
The conversation had been easy and punctuated with laughter and
smiles. She explained how her father had gotten a car and she would
love to learn to drive.

Charlie reminded her that it usually took three years even to start classes!

"Yes, that was true," she agreed and gave him a glance from the corner of her eye. "But maybe not always so long." She paused a few seconds and added, "Do you think I could learn? Are you that great of an instructor?"

Charlie smiled. "Yes, I am. You would learn quickly."

They reached Flori's family home in a half hour, and the girls gathered their things to jump out. Extensive rose gardens surrounded the one-story brown and blue stucco home. Blooms from dark blue to red filled the enclosed yard and patio with rich, fragrant scents. Vegetables and herbs in various clay pots dotted the yard, and all of this was surrounded by a fence with a gate at the street. Flori quickly scribbled her phone number on a slip of paper from her purse. "Here, here is my number." And with a smile and a flip of her long hair, this girl in the smart green dress and high heels opened the gate and disappeared down the tunnel created by a grape-draped trellis.

Charlie could faintly see her father looking out the window, and he knew the neighbors were watching. It was part of the culture of the community. Like most unmarried women, Flori lived with her family, a lively place filled with friends and family. Her father was an industrial engineer, who had invented many machines and operational designs that had been awarded government medals and accommodations. Her mother enjoyed keeping her home, caring for family and taking in sewing, a common cottage industry.

Before closing the bright blue door, Flori looked back out to the street and smiled again to see Charlie's car still there. As he pulled away from the gate, Charlie also smiled to himself. She had sparked the hope of love within Charlie's heart that even after a decade had not disappointed either of them.

Charlie had called her the next day, and they saw each other every day in April. By May, they were engaged. They married just two weeks later, in June of 1982. He and Flori bought a three-bedroom apartment in a nice section of town. They enjoyed young married life, traveling on weekends and joining friends for dinners at various restaurants after work. They had everything a young couple in Romania could hope to have, plus they also had hearts ready to welcome a baby. But after eight years, they began to understand adoption was their best way to create the family they so desired.

By 1990, in post-revolutionary Romania, Charlie anticipated the need for driving instructors and positioned himself to be prepared. The paperwork was completed and turned in to the new government before others even considered the business opportunity. It paid off financially, and Charlie was quickly a successful and respected businessman. They were able to pay off their thirty-year loan on their apartment and invest wisely. It was an exciting time after the revolution to see freedom and opportunities develop.

In this emerging new economy, money and influence were still extremely powerful. Marius's arrival in their home through a private adoption was the result of Charlie's financial success and their many influential contacts. Flori was a computer technician who continued to work for the new government. But with the arrival of Baby Marius, she began the two-year family leave from her job that the country provided for mothers to stay home and care for new babies.

Like most adoptive parents, they had devoted themselves to be attentive to every detail and choice. In the last year, Flori successfully earned her family's respect by transitioning from the office to the nursery. She was a stay-at-home mom who faithfully read and followed the Blue Book, the Romanian guide for perfect parenting of young children. Flori and her baby son were inseparable, and she enthusiastically tended to Marius's every need. She cherished and pondered in her heart his first smile, first tooth, and first steps.

Flori carefully dressed Marius for play times and walks in the parks surrounding their apartment. The stroller was new, and they were a strikingly handsome family. Charlie was tall, with dark hair and a commanding presence. He wore contemporary, European cut suits. Flori was young and beautiful, with rich, dark hair that swirled in soft waves around her shoulders. She enjoyed dressing up and wearing high heels. They took walks in the city's parks and talked with friends or chatted with business connections. Evening strolls were an expected and important aspect of social and business life in Romania. It was the way you learned what was going on in your town.

They rejoiced in this taste of freedom to meet and talk freely, to laugh with friends, and maintain and meet new contacts. They enjoyed the congratulations and admiration as they showed off their son. He was always so well-behaved and happy. Marius would smile and engage even the most serious people on these walks. His charm helped make strangers into friends. Life was good, and it only promised to get better.

This style of clothes or thinking was not the old way, but Flori and Charlie were not old. They had helped end old-style Communism with demonstrations in the squares. There had been elections, and now they felt part of the new way. Who knew what the future might include or how it might evolve? This new economic and personal freedom required tremendous adjustments. Under Communist control, citizens lived with a constant tension a misunderstood action would be considered disrespectful or the fear someone would report a careless comment. So much had changed during the nine years they had been married. Relaxing took practice.

CHAPTER 38

Bucharest, Romania
August 18, 1991

THE DAY AFTER THEY RETURNED from Ukraine, Flori and Charlie were relieved to be back in their apartment in Bucharest. Other than Flori's Aunt Cristina and Ernest, they had not shared the miraculous story with anyone else in their family. They themselves did not quite know how to understand it. They had not called anyone else on the day of the accident. After Marius was once again alive, it still seemed too overwhelmingly emotional to find the words to explain to their families over the phone. The story began with an awful accident for which they each felt enormously guilty. And how does one share with others Marius had been dead for at least eight hours, and then he had recovered so quickly? Whoever heard of such a thing? So they had not talked or communicated with family, and they had asked Flori's aunt and cousin not to share it either.

"I am ashamed to describe how our baby fell down the pipe. I don't want to cry in front of my family," Flori mentioned to Charlie over the morning coffee.

"Well, it is not a secret we need to keep. We both feel guilty, but we both worked and saved him. It will be hard to tell them. But it will be harder not to tell them."

"Yes, I know. Let's do that today and not have to think about doing it."

The first day, they visited both Flori's and Charlie's families, but the words did not come easily. Marius cleverly entertained Flori's extended family. He balanced on his tiptoes to see the flowers and squealed with delight at a yellow kitten that wandered in from the neighborhood. His charm delighted his young cousins, who showered him with kisses. So Flori's family did not initially understand the event. The couple was vague about the nature of the accident, only that Marius had been submerged, rescued, and then had been in the hospital. It was almost impossible for the family to comprehend the ordeal with Marius chasing his cousins around in Flori's parents' courtyard. They saw a completely recovered little boy. The seriousness of the accident seemed in such profound contradiction to the energetic and happy child. They understood Charlie and Flori had been upset and worried. New parents usually overreact. Cousins and aunts and uncles lifted him up and hugged him tightly and pronounced him perfectly normal.

"I cannot believe it!" Flori's sister smiled and said, "Look at him!"

The family reunion in the Mada Family yard near the summer kitchen went much the same way. They told the story simply, and few questions were asked. Charlie's family home was like a vineyard. It was a happy and comfortable place to imagine everything was going to be just fine. Flori and Charlie smiled and enjoyed themselves, but they were relieved not to have to share more.

Years ago, his parents had covered the roof of the home with scaffolding that allowed a person to climb onto the roof and reach up to pick lush clusters of grapes hanging below deep blue skies. The rest of the yard used every square inch to grow other types of vegetables and herbs. Many nights, the family gathered friends around the summer table and enjoyed the oasis they had created within the city limits. The Madas returned to their apartment happy with the day's reunions.

The next day, Flori kept an appointment with Marius's usual doctor, who listened carefully to Flori's story. For a scientist and mother, the story was a lot to understand and process.

"Flori, this does not happen, but I know you. You are someone I trust to be a truthful and intelligent mother. It is an incredible account. I believe you. Nevertheless, I would like to talk to the doctor there to confirm and consult on continued treatment."

The accident was so inconsistent with the active, adorable child in her office that the doctor called Doctor Mariana immediately. She heard the miraculous account directly from Dr. Mariana, who was delighted to hear Marius continued to be in excellent health. The doctors agreed to evaluate him for a few months with the most advanced tests and protocol available in the capital city. Flori promised to update both of the doctors with those test results and progress. The family left the office with nothing but a recommendation for continued tests with several doctors in Bucharest at The Dr. V. G. Children's Hospital.

The Madas followed through with an appointment with Dr. Gabrielle, who was the most respected neuropsychiatry specialist. Her exam and the battery of tests she ordered showed no consequences of the accident. Flori and Charlie were encouraged by all the reports that documented what they saw—Marius was in excellent health. Flori took the reports out and re-read them several times a week.

At their last visit, the respected doctor shook their hands and said, "Just keep an eye on him, and enjoy your son!"

But within their home, Flori and Charlie's watchful eyes followed and judged Marius's every move. Did he lose his balance then? Do you hear a rattle in his chest? It was exhausting to watch so carefully for a subtle, first sign of complications. And it prevented them from resuming the normal life they longed for each morning.

Charlie returned to work on September first. He continued to be more relaxed and happy than Flori had ever seen him. He talked about leaving Romania every day, most days several times. But his idea of leaving was not backed by any planning. He still didn't know where he wanted to go; in fact, he told Flori he really didn't want to go anywhere.

"Are you not happy with your work?" Flori asked.

"No, I like my work, and the business is growing. As long as Paul continues to do the classroom instruction and paperwork, I am happy to teach driving skills. I like my work. Paul is a good business partner. It is good. I am happy."

Flori could see he was happy, which made it all the more difficult to understand his continued insistence that he needed to leave the country. Charlie continued in his daily routine without the usual planning he enjoyed in anticipation of a trip. His exuberant mood, lack of planning, and continued convictions he needed to leave Romania just didn't add up, and Flori worried.

Finally, one day, as Charlie brought up the subject again, Flori said, "You decide and tell me. I do not want to talk about nothing. No place. No plan. My heart is filled with our baby. I don't have time for your empty idea. When you decide, you tell me. Until then ..." and she put her finger to her lips to show him silence. And they did not talk about it again.

CHAPTER 39

Bucharest, Romania
September 1991
Charlie

I UNDERSTAND THAT FLORI DOESN'T want to talk about leaving Romania, even for a visit somewhere. It is the "somewhere" she is upset about. But I don't know where, and so all I am left to share is what I don't know.

A young man calls and has the necessary documents to take driving lessons. He is nice, but he seems like an ordinary student and the lessons like many others I give each week. All students practice driving skills on a special track, but when they are ready, I also take them on public roads and demonstrate safe techniques. It is during one of those lessons that this young man begins talking about his great desire to go to the United States.

"It is very difficult to get a visa to go there. My friend has been trying for several years, but there is an agency nearby that organizes such trips. Would you drive me over to talk with the lady he recommended?"

I have never wanted to go to the United States. It is so large and very far away. People have told me it is expensive and so diverse in its people and land that it is difficult even to say you have been there since every region is different.

The young man keeps talking about the United States, even as I try to change the subject to discuss traveling someplace that I have been and enjoyed. He persists, "There is a lady at this agency who helps people prepare the necessary paperwork to travel to distant and interesting places. I want to talk with her."

The young man goes on and on explaining the agency provides affordable tours by renting homes in various cities where small groups could sleep for a time. Excellent Romanian style meals are available with tour guides. Members of the young man's family heard about it, and it seems like a great way to travel since he doesn't speak English. The tour guide would help navigate the language and customs too. The young man's enthusiastic conversation is contagious.

I shrug my shoulders and say, "Okay, I will take you there, and I will talk to her too." I know the address and start maneuvering through the heavy afternoon traffic. I think maybe this is more than just luck to meet a successful travel agent.

We quickly arrive at the address, and it seems like an impressive travel agency. The woman is in, and she answers our questions professionally and completely. The tour's most popular trip spends time in New York City, Cleveland, and Washington DC. Groups stay in home settings, and a guide remains with them on a hired bus for the eight-day tour.

The only difficulty is in getting a travel visa to the United States, which is the least available and most highly-desired destination. She explains the US Embassy only issues a very limited number, and it might take years.

Now, during the driving lessons, I begin to think about the United States. Why would they make it difficult for me to visit? Why would people spend a great deal of money to go to this country? What do they see that is that important? The young man finished the school, and I never see him again.

Then the next group of students arrives, and on the first day, I am teaching a young woman named Andrea. Soon she is sharing how much she wants to travel to the United States. She explains that she has heard of a travel agency that helps people apply for visa and travel documentation. I nod, and she is surprised!

"Do you know of this agency?" she asked.

I am shocked. In all the years of giving lessons, no one has ever initiated conversations about traveling so intensely, and now two have shown the same interest in the same agency.

"Yes, I know the agency, and I know the lady. I was there just last week. I will take you there." And as simply as that, I return for a second visit to the same agency. The lady to whom I had spoken before is again at the office. She is the owner, and she patiently explains how their tours work. It is expensive, and I see that the young woman does not have the money, but it is affordable for me. The owner is impressed that the cost does not decrease my interest, so she continues to warn of the necessary patience required to wait sometimes several years for a tourist visa.

My interest and competitive spirit increase during the second visit. I think maybe it is possible for us to get visas. It is difficult, but it does not seem impossible. The United States is the premier destination, and this woman encourages me to try to go there. There are beautiful pamphlets showing blue skies, white clouds, towering skyscrapers, and glorious monuments. I pick some out to take home. They are interesting and something that I can share and discuss with future driving students once I return from such an impressive trip. Such conversations are part of the job of building a business. People who find you interesting and competent also recommend you to friends.

But my motivation is more than casual curiosity, because I have a growing confidence I am being guided by circumstances. I am not sure where or when we are to go, but I have always been sure I would know. This second visit gives me peace and confidence that this is what I am to do. I gather up the documents necessary to complete the applications for visas and bring them home to Flori.

CHAPTER 40

Bucharest, Romania
September 1991
Flori

I AM DUMBSTRUCK. CHARLIE COMES home and puts a few pretty brochures on the table, and suddenly he thinks he knows where he wants to go. This morning he has no idea; now he is certain! Why is there no discussion and comparison of places? How can he go out this morning without an idea and return so very certain? Of course, I really don't want to go anywhere, do I?

Real papers and real visas create real fears that my husband is in the middle of an emotional breakdown. His behavior is unexplainable. He has never in ten years expressed any interest in going to the United States.

I pick up the brochures of pretty skies and clouds. There are clouds and blue skies everywhere. "Charlie, we have everything here. Why do you want to go? Our last vacation was a nightmare, and I am not even over that yet. Why do you want to go so much?"

"I don't know. I know I am supposed to leave Romania. Why should I not want to go and see new parts of the world and meet new people? I will be gone for less than two weeks. It is only a holiday trip. I feel like I must do this."

I begin to feel tingling sensations in my hands. I am frightened and deeply alarmed by the changes in Charlie. All I want is to return to our normal routine after the accident. This travel talk is just chaotic, confusing static. Charlie is intent on going, and I do not feel it is safe for him to go alone.

Charlie comes over and takes my hand. "Come with me. I want you to come with me. I don't want to go alone. In fact, it would please me very much if you say you will go also." I feel lost in such an idea. I don't want to go. I don't want him to go alone. Gone are some of my fears that the problem is within our marriage, but there is clearly a problem within Charlie. I find his excited and happy mood to be surprisingly annoying.

CHAPTER 41

Bucharest, Romania
October 1991

FLORI TOOK LONG WALKS DURING the fall days. Walking with other mothers pushing strollers and chasing babies, she privately debated her best strategies to deal with whatever Charlie had going on in his head. Nearby, Marius continued to thrive: running, jumping, and trying to catch the falling, colored leaves. Still, it was difficult not to be afraid of everything. Was Marius climbing too high on the park equipment? Was that his cough? What was on the ground she couldn't see that might make her son trip or fall? And mixed up in this anxiety was Charlie's plan.

To buy more time, Flori agreed to meet the travel agent and learn more about the tour. She was not anxious to have a full-out argument about the whole crazy plan. She hoped Charlie would snap back into his comfortable, familiar patterns of behavior. So Flori cautiously dressed and drove with Charlie to the America Tour Travel Agency and listened to the owner's presentation. They investigated all the necessary steps. Flori wrote them all down, hoping that as the list lengthened and complications were so easily calculated, Charlie would also understand the challenges and abandon this obsession.

First, they would need to pay nine hundred dollars plus 160,000 lei to complete all the necessary paperwork. The visa would be an additional fee. She began to understand the cost of the vacation would equal twelve years' salary from her government job. They had these resources, but spending part of their savings on an unexpected trip was surprising to Flori. It added to her anxiety about the state of Charlie's decision-making. He was a wise and conservative investor. They had the savings because he did not spend money carelessly. He usually would have planned such a trip far in advance with much research. This quick decision marked a real change in his personality, and it continued to disturb Flori.

While they were there, Flori picked up several nice pamphlets about Hungary. The pictures looked interesting, and it wasn't that far away. Flori suggested they arrange a trip to Hungary in hopes that would satisfy him. However, Charlie had no peace in that plan, and he did not want to follow false steps. He wanted to apply for a visa to go to the United States.

Flori was still only sharing with her aunt during long conversations on the phone. Her aunt clarified Flori's resolve. If they did get visas, Flori felt she should accompany Charlie. She felt he might just disappear and never return, not because she doubted he would want to return to her and Marius or Romania, but because he was acting so differently. She worried he might act recklessly. He might leave the tour or wander off and get lost. The possibilities of foul play or violence due to his new trusting manner played themselves out in her imagination. Something had profoundly changed, and it left Charlie unpredictable. She decided if he went, she must also go.

She began to struggle with the unbearable decision she might need to leave Marius with her aunt for those eight days. If during the trip Charlie's erratic behavior got worse, or there was another more intense crisis, she needed to be free to take care of him and not also be taking care of a toddler. It was a gut-wrenching choice only made possible when her aunt agreed to come and live in their apartment during their trip. The women agreed since visas were so difficult to obtain, perhaps all their worry and plans were for nothing. Flori continued to hope the decision to go would be one she would never have to make.

Flori tried to engage Charlie in the planning of packing and travel details. She asked him questions about the possible temperatures and what they would be expected to wear. By acting like she was anxious to go to the United States, she hoped she more would better understand him, but it gave her little insight. At times, Charlie just seemed childishly naive about the consequences and difficulties of this adventure. She was used to Charlie bringing home six maps and studying the route they would take for a trip. He would talk to people and research places of interest and tips about where to stay and eat. For this big trip, he was unengaged in the details.

"Oh, it is a tour. They will take care of each day. We will go where they take us," he stated one night.

She was speechless. Charlie continued to bounce in the door, swing her around, kiss her, and tickle Marius. He was kind and patient. As her anxiety increased, his decreased. So Flori went along with the plans, gathering all the necessary papers and applications to go to the United States. Her continued, great hope was that they would be denied visas. If they applied and were denied, they could not apply again for a year, and they would have another year to reconsider. He would be pleased with her, and perhaps time would solve the problem.

It had only been a few weeks since the accident and the extreme stress they had each endured. Other than his excessive joy, in all other ways, Charlie seemed stable and normal. But this obsession and the manner in which he was behaving about this trip were deeply troubling. Then again, who would even listen if she complained her husband was too happy?

Charlie continued to be ecstatic. He jumped out of bed and sang his way through breakfast and out the door to work. He anticipated something wonderful happening each day. His undefined need to leave Romania was being fulfilled. His wife was showing interest in the adventure, and that seemed perfect. He had doubted she would leave Marius, but she had agreed. She had chosen to go with him, and he was very happy.

Although everyone warned him not to get his hopes up that they could get visas, he believed it was probable. The Madas followed through with the paperwork, liquidated assets to cover the expenses, and made an appointment for their interview at the American Embassy for October 10, 1991.

The night before their appointment, they sat at the apartment table and organized all their papers. Charlie had driven over to locate the embassy and decide on the best parking. He was filled with bubbling optimism, while Flori looked around her apartment and reflected on how perfect it all seemed. Charlie's smile and boyish excitement were to some degree contagious, so Flori enjoyed the affection her participation evoked. They were on this adventure together, even though they each had an entirely different definition of adventure.

CHAPTER 42

Bucharest, Romania
October 10, 1991

As Charlie and Flori approached the American Embassy, he saw one of his friends standing near some large, black, American cars. Charlie explained to Flori that he was a driver for the consul. "What good luck to see him," they whispered to each other.

"Charlie! You look so good. It has been too long! What are you doing here?" his friend asked after introductions to Flori.

"We are here for an interview for tourist visas," Charlie answered.

His friend laughed. "They don't even give me and my wife a tourist visa! I cannot be of any help to you. Good luck, my friend."

Charlie teased him back, and they parted with friendly laughs.

Since they had been given a specific appointment time, the Madas were surprised to see over one hundred and fifty people in a line near the fence. At first, they didn't believe it was the visa line, but military guards issued them numbers 166 and 167 and then directed them to the end of the line. Fifty people at a time were allowed through the fence and into the waiting room for personal appointments.

Although other people in line were tense and avoided personal conversations, Charlie was unusually relaxed. The line's somber mood did match Flori's attitude. She realized she was the only one in line with a desperate desire for failure, while her husband was the only one in line with a certain hope of success. She looked at his casual body language, smile, and confidence. He looked entirely different from anyone else. She wondered how he could seem so unaware of the situation and probable decision. How would he react if they were denied? Would there be an outburst? She didn't want any trouble from either the Americans or the Romanians. She looked at the tall, armed, young American Marines and held her breath.

Once they were admitted inside the embassy, the atmosphere was even more serious than the line outside. There was a man at the far end of the room whose hair flew up each time he pounded a large stamp down on the pad. Charlie made a face mocking him. Flori tried silently to tell him to stop. Charlie continued joking around while they waited for their names to be called. She worried his behavior was so inappropriate they would be asked to leave. Flori was increasingly confused about her feelings. She did not want to win the prize and get the golden visa, and yet she didn't want Charlie's bizarre behavior to be the reason why they didn't. That would confirm her fears he was having a breakdown.

"Numbers 166 and 167. Mada," a middle-aged woman called, and they followed her to a wooden desk in a small, semi-private office.

"Why do you want to go?" she asked.

"We wish to go see the United States," Charlie answered vaguely.

"Will you take your child?"

"No, he will stay here with my aunt," answered Flori.

"Do you have business there?"

"No, no business."

The lady sneezed very energetically with a funny hoot in the middle.

"God bless you!" Charlie quickly said.

"I wish you luck," she gave the traditional greeting.

"My luck depends on you." Charlie laughed and flashed a big friendly smile. She also laughed. The Madas and the lady continued to have a conversation about small matters. It didn't seem like much of an interview to decide who would receive a visa. And then quickly, and totally unexpectedly, she loudly stamped their application and looked them directly in the eyes. "Go over there and pay for your visas."

It was over that quickly.

Charlie and Flori looked at each other. Both were in shock for different reasons. To be the ones selected, the ones approved, created a glorious rush of adrenaline! They had won the grand prize! They hugged each other with pride. But when Charlie presented the papers at the next desk, Flori immediately was conflicted between winning and losing.

The older man at the window said, as he took their money, "Oh, you won the prize today. These are only the sixth and seventh visas approved today out of 167 applications!"

Flori's heart pounded in her chest, and the lump in her throat became more intense. The impossible had become true. Now she would have to choose to follow through with her agreement to go with Charlie and leave Marius behind, or she would refuse to go. Whatever she decided, she knew that Charlie would leave.

Charlie was more than happy for the two of them. He had understood getting visas had been unlikely, but he also had a confident hope that the way would be made clear for him to follow this unexplainable quest that had seemingly been planted in his soul. He hadn't imagined it wouldn't happen. He didn't know what he would have done if the visas had not been given to them. He had that much confidence.

Once they had paid and signed their signatures, a couple behind them pushed ahead, and the door to the outside opened for them. They each took a long breath of chilly, Romanian air.

"Eight days in the United States. What an amazing adventure we have!"

Flori looked over at his smiling face. She wondered how he could not know how difficult this choice was for her. He had heard her say she would go when it seemed so unlikely they would be allowed to travel. Did he not understand all of that? But it was clear he did not. He looked like a schoolboy hearing about an unexpected holiday. "Eight days," Flori thought. "I can do eight days. He must not go alone."

Charlie began to plan how to liquidate various holdings to arrange for the cost. He could sell a car, which would bring in 50,000

LEI. When it didn't sell immediately, he sold a rather new stereo system and some car parts. Charlie had connections to get good prices for items that were difficult to purchase, so he began to make the calls and sell off unnecessary items. They hoped the car would sell before they left. But Charlie's relaxed attitude, when he was offered so much less than he expected for the car and the extraordinarily poor exchange rate, were uncharacteristic. Flori watched all of this with continued confusion and frustration.

CHAPTER 43

The National Bank of Romania Bucharest, Romania
November 1991
Flori

WE CONTINUE TO PREPARE SLOWLY for the trip, and Charlie remains somewhat indifferent to all that we need to do. With only two weeks left before our departure, we still have not converted the Romanian lei into American dollars. Charlie hopes the exchange rate might improve, but with time running out to departure day, I have gone ahead with plans to make the exchange.

"But why doesn't Charlie go to the bank and exchange the money?" Aunt Cristina asks. She has arrived a week before our departure to enjoy a visit and prepare to take care of Marius.

"Oh, he is desperate to complete all the preparations necessary for work. I know where to go, and I can do this. I want to make sure we have enough cash."

Aunt Cristina glances over at me and raises her eyebrows. "Are you planning to go shopping when you are in the United States?"

"No, not shopping." I flash her a smile and sit down on my bed where Aunt Cristina is folding Marius's clean clothes. She does so slowly and lovingly. Aunt Cristina has a special love for Marius, having seen him in the bed without life. So now she doesn't tire of watching this lively, curious toddler. She makes him laugh and spoils him like a grandmother does a grandson.

Aunt Cristina stops and looks over. "No, I didn't think shopping. You want to take enough money because you are still worried."

"Yes, I want to have enough to face whatever might happen. I want to know we can get on a plane and come home. If there is a problem with Charlie, money is all I will be able to depend on in the United States."

My aunt reaches over and wraps her arms around me. I do not protest. "Let's have tea."

I look in to see Marius is still napping and carefully close his bedroom door. He will not go with me today. Marius is an exceptionally well-behaved baby, and often his smiles and waves make waiting in long, Romanian lines easier. People are drawn to him, and often strangers play with him. Then they pull old and tattered photographs of their son or grandson at the same age from their worn, leather wallets.

These last few weeks, I do not mind when time moves slowly. I am happy just enjoying Marius discovering the world of playgrounds and parks. Our son thinks twigs or round stones are treasures to save and bring home to show to his daddy. My apprehension and sadness grow as the departure date nears.

Today, I explain to Aunt Cristina I have to take several buses to get to the National Bank. We agree Marius should not come with me. We briefly go over the tour schedule in the United States. "I will take care of Marius like he is my own son. You go and take care of Charlie. And take care of yourself." It is overwhelmingly comforting to understand each other without long, serious discussions. I tiptoe out of the kitchen door waving a silent goodbye to Aunt Cristina and our empty teacups.

The bus ride seems to go quickly enough. The stately, stone building looks important enough to be a bank in any European capital. I climb the stairs and am pleased there are only three people ahead of me. All three are middle-aged businessmen. We all stand along the stone railings on the left side of the descending steps. Others form a long line behind me. The line grows as young couples, dressed like students with books in hand, join us. Later come older couples who might never have traveled beyond their mother country. Most fashionable business people wear blue suits with white shirts.

The morning wears on, and my hope fades that I can quickly make the exchange and get back home to be with Marius.

I look up at the blue sky. "Stay in the moment," I remind myself. The day is pleasant for the season in Bucharest, but just standing in line on the stairs looking up at three massive doors is discouraging. By mid-morning, the business people are grumbling. They doubt the bank has any American dollars.

"Last week it was the same. No dollars. And yet they let us wait here," the young man behind me says to anyone who is listening. "Who will do business with us if our government cannot acquire an adequate amount of dollars?"

The young man's frank statement is a sign of the changing times, but it still surprises me. He is comfortable criticizing the government in an open space among strangers. What is he? Ten years younger than me? He was not an adult before the revolution. And here he is in his dark gray suit with international newspapers under his arm, expecting to engage in international business transactions. He is annoyed by the inconvenience of waiting. I smile. Rapid political change and the resulting social adjustment can be confusing at times and amusing at others.

A few of the travelers begin to leave the line. "Maybe the banker's brother is in the dark money exchange. No money here, but for a less favorable rate, lots of money available in the back room."

Another down the stairs agreed, "It is a conspiracy to control business."

I listen and don't say anything. I am fourth in line, and if anyone gets dollars today, I believe I will. It is difficult to think such a large bank would allow a line to form and have patrons stay outside all day if they could not accommodate the need for currency exchange.

A man about thirty years old climbs to the middle of the steps. He is not remarkable looking, but he walks with confidence and catches my eye. I am startled when he stops at my side. He doesn't say a word. I cannot help looking over at him, thinking perhaps this is someone Charlie or I know. But I don't recognize him, so my second thought is that maybe he is trying to cut into the line.

He is nice looking in an ordinary way, confident but quiet. Still, I hold the large bag packed with our cash a little closer to my body. Looking me in the eyes, he says, "I have come today because I have to exchange the money with you."

I am taken aback. The man does not seem like a physical threat, but his selecting me in a long line of hopeful people raises my suspicions immediately. I wonder if perhaps he has seen a young woman alone, and he has picked me out to rob me.

"No, thank you. I will wait." I wave my hand without a smile toward the large, closed bank doors.

The man again looks me right in the eyes, and without any nervous or suspicious body language speaks to me very directly.

"I will exchange with you at the same rate. The bank doesn't have money today."

Why would this stranger approach me? Perhaps he has picked me out as an inexperienced tourist who would not know the difference between real and fake American dollars. Perhaps I look like the most gullible of all the people in the line.

I repeat, "No, I will wait for the bank."

Immediately he says, "The bank doesn't have the money to exchange today."

Mutely, I just stare at him.

He continues, "I will wait for you." With that, the young man quickly walks back down the steps, passing dozens of people in line who are hoping to do exactly what I am also there to do. Jumping the two-foot high black, wrought iron fence, he stands in the shade of the trees next to a large, ornate, office building.

I watch him and am relieved he has gone away. *I think it is okay with me if you wait over there. You are not a worry to me, and you can wait as long as you wish. And why if it was such a great deal, didn't you offer it to someone else in line? Why wait over there by the building?* Occasionally I glance over to see if he has left or approached someone else. But he is in the same place. It is odd and makes me feel uncomfortable.

The sun rises higher. I ask the man behind me if he could save my spot, and I will run and get us some fruit or cheese to eat for lunch. He agrees, and I give the large doors at the top of the steps a quick glance. I don't want to risk not being there if the doors open up and the bank begins business. There doesn't seem to be any movement or change in the behavior of the guards. I dash into a small store and pick up some fruit, bread, and water.

As I round the corner, someone roughly bumps me, causing me to lose my balance. Immediately a half-dozen, young men surround me. Their aggressive movements are threatening. I am alarmed! It is common knowledge that bands of criminals rob citizens even on busy streets. They blend in with crowds and suddenly, on a silent signal, swarm around a target. Then they swiftly rob or assault their victim. I had heard news stories of citizens who were cut with a knife badly enough to loosen their grips on their bags, only to have the handle of the bag also cut. Within seconds the criminals would disperse, disappearing back into the crowd. I look around for help and see none.

"Are you here to exchange? We will exchange with you." The gang's leader speaks in a distinct dialect, and the other men laugh and move in closer. I look around, but none of the people walking on the street make eye contact with me. My hand tightens on the bag packed with our cash. A hundred thoughts race through my head. As I try to assess the real danger and come up with the best plan, the mysterious man steps up beside me and takes my arm. He doesn't say a word of rebuke to the gang who suddenly become silent, step back and allow us to pass. We walk safely to the street corner and across to the bank.

The encounter shakes me. My heart races and steals my breath, leaving me unable to even whisper a thank you to my savior. If not for this stranger, I would have been robbed of all of our money and possibly injured by an attack. By the time I stop shaking, the man has crossed back across the street, jumped the fence, and is once again leaning against the building. I return to the line, and for the rest of the afternoon, I occasionally glance over to see if he leaves or talks to someone else. He does not.

At four o'clock the guards announce the bank is closing its doors for the day. As I turn to walk down the steps, feeling all the aches and pains of my day of standing in the sun, the strange man approaches me again. I start to thank him, but he interrupts, "I told you the bank doesn't have the money. I came to exchange with you. I have to exchange the money with you. I will come back tomorrow."

"I will come back tomorrow to see if the bank has money." I am still upset by the day's events, and the noble, but very strange, behavior of this man is confusing. I sit on the back bench of the bus and watch the parade of landmarks in reverse. I let my head fall back on the seat. What would have happened if the strange man had not come up and saved me from the young men? Could he be one of them? Was this a large trick? He didn't look like them, and he seemed relaxed and almost kind. Why had he approached only me when the line was long with disappointed people? I need to talk to Charlie about all of this.

Exhausted from the physical exertion and the very confusing conversations I had with the stranger, I wonder why nothing seems simple anymore. Before Marius's accident, days followed days. They were ordinary, without drama or stress. Now each day is filled with difficult decisions. Decisions that became even more difficult and confusing with never-ending oddities, twists, and coincidences.

When he gets home, Charlie listens carefully, expressing his anger about the gang and appreciation for the man's protective actions. We make a plan for the next day.

"Ahhh, let's remember how easy it will be to exchange dollars to lei's. When we return from the USA, we should bring leftover dollars home to exchange with someone else."

Charlie looks over at me, overwhelmingly optimistic that all of this is going to end well. He pats my hand. "Okay, if the bank doesn't have money by noon, bring the man to our living room. I will come home at noon tomorrow and meet you both at our apartment and decide if we want to exchange. Unfortunately, I have students all day tomorrow. But I can take an hour lunch at one o'clock."

"All right. That is what we will do. But I don't believe the same mystery man will be there tomorrow. Finding someone else interested in a money exchange is easy. There are many people just waiting in line who wish to do so." I close my eyes and think of the extended bus trip leaving very early in the morning again in just a few hours.

"It is okay if he is not there. I will just eat lunch and return to work. We need to exchange. Why doesn't the bank have money?" Within minutes, Charlie's breathing gives testimony his confidence outweighed any stress, and he is asleep. I, however, begin to think all over again about the stranger. *Why doesn't he just go to the bank and make an exchange? Why does he not approach other people in the line? How does he have time just to wait all day for me? Will we be able to tell if the dollars he brings are real and not fake?* I toss and turn in dreams of me running and not getting to where Charlie is waiting for me.

The next morning, I arrive at the bank just twenty minutes later than the day before. The bus trips are crowded and unpleasant, and I am even more disappointed that I am at the end of the morning exchange line. Then I hear the stranger's voice close beside me. "Hello. I came back. I have to exchange money with you. The bank doesn't have the money today." The same man calmly explains his mission. "I have to exchange money with you." Again I am suspicious why he is so singularly focused on exchanging with me rather than with anyone else in line who could give him a quick and fair deal.

But the stranger is calm and pleasant. Smiling, I explain my husband's plan to meet him at our apartment at lunch. To my surprise, he agrees. He hustles down the steps, jumps the fence, and waits, leaning against the same building as the day before. I patiently wait to learn if the bank has American money. I turn and look up at the three bank doors. There are two and a half hours to get through those doors, or I will take this mysterious man home to meet Charlie.

During the morning, hours creep by giving me too much time to wonder if our plan is safe. Why has no one in the line entered into the conversation, acknowledged the man's offer, or shared an opinion about the wisdom of working with him? It is as though no one else has heard his offer.

The line never advances. It does not look like anyone will be getting into the bank, and rumors swirl up and down the steps that the bank is again without U.S. dollars. Great disappointment ripples through the line. At noon, the man appears and asks if I am ready. We return to our apartment on the buses and meet Charlie just as we planned. Charlie quickly assesses the stranger. He is average height and weight, brown hair with graying on the sides. He has no accent and offers a straight smile and business-like manner. We do not ask his name, but he explains he worked in the USA and had saved US dollars. We enjoy cups of coffee and sandwiches. Then the man begins to discuss what it is like living in the United States.

I listen politely, but my headache returns and interferes with my ability to concentrate. I wonder if Marius is still asleep, and I want to excuse myself to go and get him soon. The pain of leaving our son is a growing ache. Watching Charlie's enthusiasm almost seems like watching his disloyalty. Silently, I begin to question Charlie's devotion to our son and even perhaps to me. A headache is hard to ignore.

Finally, Charlie looks at his watch and bemoans, "Whoa, I need to get back. A student is waiting for me."

We all stand up. Then the strange man says the strangest thing. "When you go to the United States, you will be with a group of Protestant people." He must have seen our astonished look, and so he repeats more seriously and firmly, "When you go to the United States, you will be with a group of Protestant people. You will hear about Jesus. It doesn't matter what is happening—do not depart from them."

I look at the American dollars on the table and worry they are fake. I laugh and think the man is even stranger than I thought. *What's he talking about? We are going on an eight-day tour, a vacation. I am not going to be interested in religious matters. I don't want to talk to absurd, religious people.* I marvel that obstacles to our departure are being removed in the most unusual ways. Life didn't use to seem so strange, and I again wonder what we have gotten ourselves into.

After both men leave, I happily go in and swing Marius out of his crib, comb his hair, and enjoy his emerging vocabulary. "Yes! Let's go to the park and play!" I laugh, kissing him on his forehead. But inside, my heart counts the days, and it once again breaks in two.

CHAPTER 44

Bucharest, Romania to USA
December 2, 1991

FLORI AND CHARLIE'S NEIGHBOR CALLED out to them that morning as they carried their bags into the elevator.

"You are going to America today, aren't you?"

"Yes, yes, we are going! Please look in on Cristina and offer her help with building information, yes?"

"Of course," the neighbor smiled, "but you have a very important person on your flight. Do you know who is going with you to New York?"

Charlie shook his head. The neighbor didn't offer any details, as he was waiting for Flori's answer. Flori shrugged her shoulders to indicate she didn't know either.

"Well, Monk Argatu from the Monastery of Cernica!"

The priest was a celebrity in Romania. He was widely respected when word spread that after his blessings, miracles follow, and demons are cast out. He often preached about the love of Jesus and served the community with food programs and elder care. His excellent reputation resulted in easy fundraising. He was considered a good, generous, and powerful man. Even Flori and Charlie had sought his blessing during the time they desired a family and were not successful conceiving a child. Recently, there had been alarming reports of his possible poisoning by Communist agents. He now suffered serious health problems, and it was a big story in Bucharest and the entire country. He was reported near death for three days. Unable to go to the hospital in fear of continued attacks, his body had been laid out at the Monastery. His apparent recovery and travel plans had not been so widely reported.

The Madas arrived at the airport, and there stood the 78-year-old monk just feet from them in the airport waiting room. It would have been difficult to miss him, as he was dressed in dark robes, with deep-set eyes, a long white beard and the same toothless smile they remembered from their short visit with him years earlier. A small, well-worn leather satchel was next to his feet. Two aides stood nearby, rather nervously looking around at each new face in the waiting room.

Charlie approached the monk and warmly greeted him. Flori joined him and briefly told him that their prayers had been answered with the adoption of Marius. The old man had difficulty hearing, but he was good at reading lips. They thanked him for his blessing. The attending aides listened carefully and seemed to relax when they overheard the conversation. Charlie talked to them and learned because the monk was traveling alone, they were concerned. Charlie offered to carry his small bag and to watch over him. The aide alluded to his poor health and that he had recently miraculously recovered.

"Yes, yes. I will take care of him. He will be with me. Just as he takes care of the people, I will watch over him." The offer of service was punctuated with Charlie's warm smile and laugh. Charlie was dressed in an excellent camelhair coat and hat. His broad, strong frame created quite an air of strength and confidence. Both aides looked enormously relieved as they said their goodbyes with embraces and kisses.

The flight passed relatively quickly for a transatlantic flight. Charlie and the monk spoke of all that had happened during the last thirty years in Romania. The monk was intelligent and well-informed. He was well-known to have helped many good people leave Romania, saving their lives or the lives of their sons. Influential families gave generously to his fundraising for the Orthodox Monastery close to Jerusalem. A young doctor, whom Monk Argatu had helped, was sponsoring his visit to the US. He was going there to offer prayers and communion. The bond between the young doctor and the old

Romanian monk seemed very strong, and Charlie looked forward to meeting him.

In their conversations, Charlie found unusual peace. His heart that had raced before the take-off had beat slower after Monk Argatu reassured him, "Don't worry, my son, I prayed. I promise all on this plane will land safely. Be free of fear." And Charlie had felt a freedom from fear. Perhaps he felt it for the first time since Marius's accident. He liked sitting near the monk. He was pleased he could serve this man.

"I may not be allowed to get off this plane. They may prevent me from disembarking." Monk Argatu rearranged his robe and rope belt. He looked up and let out a soft, resigned sigh.

"No, they will not do that. I will be here for you," Charlie smiled.

Monk Argatu smiled back, his eyes twinkling.

During the flight, Flori and Charlie slept or read or enjoyed small talk. Flori was the first to see the lights on the distant shore and then the tall buildings. As they circled and got closer, even her excitement increased. The city was filled with flowing rivers of bright, light-filled energy. There were wide highways of moving cars stretched out in every direction, on one side red lights, and on the other side there were white headlights. She hoped this would be a great visit, short and sweet.

The plane landed on time and safely as prayer-promised. Immediately after the plane taxied to a stop at the gate at John F. Kennedy Airport in New York, they heard an announcement, "Passengers, please remain in your seats. Monk Argatu, please report to the captain."

Monk Argatu looked at Charlie. His smile faded, and he seemed resigned.

Charlie stood up. "I will go with you."

Without smiles, the two men slowly walked to the front of the plane while the rest of the passengers prepared to leave from the plane's rear door. Flori waited in her seat, straining to see what was happening.

"I am Argatu."

"No one called for you," the airline representatives stated.

"I heard it also. You called for him," Charlie said.

"No. No. He can go!" The young man with the clipboard near the pilot's cabin smiled. Flori was shocked to see both men returning. She had also heard the announcement.

"I think they were afraid of your bodyguard! Charlie, you look very intimidating."

But the monk had remained calm. "God is with me." He smiled and shook Charlie's hand. "Thank you, my son. God must have sent you for that moment."

Charlie laughed. "Ask the doctor if he can help us if we want to stay a little longer to see important things."

The monk nodded his head and said, "I'll see." He smiled, and his eyes continued to twinkle.

Flori's ears tingled. *Stay a little longer?* Charlie had never indicated to her in any way he was interested in staying longer. She was sure he had not thought of it, as he had not prepared their finances for a longer stay. And they had left their son. Her nervousness about his mental state increased. She didn't say anything to him. There would be time to sort this all out. Once they had passed through the gate, Charlie continued to carry the elderly monk's bag. Charlie's tall stature and the old man's fragile physical condition were an odd picture when the young doctor approached them. They quickly exchanged greetings and the intriguing story of the phantom announcement.

Monk Argatu expressed his gratitude for Charlie and Flori's attention and care. Doctor Virgil, who looked about thirty years old, thanked them also. Charlie asked, "Can you help us if we decide to stay longer and see additional things here?"

"Of course, of course," the doctor agreed and shared his phone number.

CHAPTER 45

New York City, New York
December 2, 1991

EVEN WITHOUT SPEAKING ENGLISH, FLORI and Charlie were able to find their luggage and get through immigration and customs. The touring company had representatives holding the company's logo on small signs just past the gate, and so they boarded a small van and joined other Romanian tourists. The touring company's modest house was in one of the outer boroughs, and it served as a guest home for travelers. Shortly after their arrival there, dinner was announced. A group of about ten adults gathered around the table, which was set with a traditional, Romanian meal. Eating in the United States with six strangers was an interesting social and political experience.

Charlie wondered, "Who are these people with means to travel to the United States? Were they active in the old government or the new?"

"We have no idea what they support and to whom they may report." Flori made a gesture showing her "lips were sealed." Smart, young Romanians still understood the need to have some caution. No one was certain what forces might be planning unexpected changes to the new government or even how the present course would evolve. History was told in pubs and around family dinner tables with the raw emotion of present tense.

Just a few years earlier in the fall of 1989, Romania had a short and violent overthrow of the Communist government of President Ceausescu. It had been a time when bold and courageous young people from Poland to Hungary had demonstrated for more representative governments. Conditions were harsh in Romania under Communism.

Throughout the late 1970s and 1980s, President Ceausescu created a government deeply-rooted in the spectacle of himself and his family's accomplishments, activities, and interests. Weekly shows in stadiums or on streets in different cities were dedicated to him, his wife, and the Communist Party. He spent lavishly for his personal projects, while children suffered malnutrition and the country had the highest infant mortality rate in Europe. Poor neighborhoods were destroyed to construct monuments. Libraries were emptied and then filled with works praising his wisdom and policies. Food, gas, and heat were rationed and either extremely expensive or difficult to find. The Secret Police paid friends and neighbors to be informants against anyone who criticized the President or his family. Everything that was said could be reported. Citizens were watched for any level of disrespect. The tension was everywhere, because no one had hope for justice if arrests were made. The balance of living a normal life and the uncertainty created by constant suspicion were always uncomfortable. Through luck and caution, the Madas had dodged false informers and random investigations.

During 1989, Charlie and Flori participated in demonstrations with thousands of Romanians in the squares of Bucharest. Everyone desired freedom of speech and self-determination, or at least they would be satisfied with Communist leaders who were less self-indulgent. By doing so, the Madas had risked more than they probably understood at the time. Within three days President Ceausescu had been tried and executed. The National Salvation Front was formed, and the difficult business of holding elections and becoming a better country began.

These experiences had developed a powerful and confident attitude in young adults. Conversations during park walks gave hope to many who wanted to work hard and have the possibility of greater rewards. But with this freedom, Charlie and Flori also had understood the change in policies and personal values might result in fewer babies being available for adoption. After years desiring a family, they had decided to follow through quickly with the applications for an adoption. Marius was an answer to their hearts' desires. Sitting in New York City with strangers, Flori and Charlie ate a good meal around two large tables, avoiding any controversial topic and showing photographs of Marius to everyone. Romanians loved nice plump, thriving babies, so Marius was a safe topic for their dinner conversations.

Shortly after the meal was over, Charlie disappeared for about ten minutes. Flori found the group lively and pleasant in conversation. Flori began to relax and think this holiday would pass quickly and be a pleasant memory.

Once Flori and Charlie met back in their simple but adequate bedroom, Charlie explained he had called and talked to Doctor Virgil, and the young doctor agreed to meet them the next day. He had even suggested they meet at a subway station near his house. Flori was non-committal that evening, preferring to go to sleep rather than to try to reason with Charlie about a plan that seemed unreasonable to her. She decided to wait and discuss it the next morning.

After breakfast, Charlie brought up his plan to leave the group and find the doctor from the airport. The group was bringing out the last of the suitcases from the house. Flori looked at Charlie. His intensity confounded her. *Why this intense interest in the doctor?*

She smiled at Charlie and said, "But we are all getting into the van to leave New York, Charlie. Is there time?"

Charlie turned and walked over nearer the van driver. Flori caught the eye of one of the women with whom she had made friends, and Flori moved closer to the women's circle near the hostess of the travel home. She hoped Charlie would see her and understand she wanted to stay with this group. Flori was listening to a middle-aged woman talk about her last trip to New York and the shopping on Fifth Avenue, when a commotion began near where the suitcases were being loaded into the van. Charlie was in the middle of it, insisting the tour guide drop them off at a train station so they could meet the young doctor again. His voice was getting louder and louder, and his hands moved from his head to his heart to motions of exasperation. "I just want to meet with him and talk with him."

"No, you cannot just go off and meet him to talk. If you do that, you will miss the whole guided tour. You will not be able to meet up with us again. We will not be in this area again." Charlie continued to try to persuade the guide there must be a way for him to meet with the young Romanian doctor for one conversation and then meet up with the group later in the day. The tour guide's frustration grew as Charlie stopped listening to his protests and continued to insist there might be a way.

The guide threw up his hands and shrugged. "Yes, I will change my route and leave you at a subway station. But then we are done." And to emphasize that point, when they reached the subway station, the guide quickly took their luggage out of the van and tossed it onto the curb. In the drama of the moment, any directions for a place to meet the van before it headed for Washington, DC were lost. Flori could see the reflection of her own disorientated and worried face in the van's back window. The middle-aged woman looked back at her, giving her a little wave before covering her mouth with her gloved hand as the tour group's van disappeared around a corner.

Flori was stunned. She didn't have time to wave back. She looked at Charlie and wondered why he was being so insistent about seeing the doctor again. What was so important that so suddenly they had left the tour with little hope of ever meeting up with them? She had just witnessed what she had exactly feared. She had come with Charlie because she knew this irrational and unexpected decision-making could result in Charlie's just disappearing. She looked at him as he was fanatically trying to call the number the doctor had scribbled on a scrap of paper.

This is the moment for which she knew she had needed to come. But the reality of leaving the tour group within the first day shocked her. What could and what should she do? Although Charlie was acting in a very alarming and impetuous manner, he did not seem crazy. Should she make a scene, call the police, and seek help? Or should she let Charlie do this his way and let her husband follow whatever force was driving him?

And suddenly the choice was natural. Her choice would be her husband. She looked at the handsome face she loved and thought, *I*

love you Charlie, and I will go with you. I will go, not because I under-
stand, or I am comfortable. I will go with you because I love you.

Charlie had listened and trusted her. When he pulled Marius
up and out of the pipe, Charlie had given her back their son. And
now she needed to help Charlie heal, so she could give their son
back his father. The three of them were meant to be a family. They
would be a family who would stand by and protect each other. She
was not going to leave one behind. She would not settle for two-
thirds of the family. The whole family would survive. If Charlie continued to insist he had to follow this force that seemed to drive him,
she would go also.

She closed her eyes and squeezed his arm, "What do we do from
here?"

CHAPTER 46

New York City, New York
December 3, 1991, morning
Flori

WE HAVE BEEN LEFT ON a corner near iron fences and a green sign marking the stairway down to the dark rumbling of the subway. Around us, long lines of yellow taxi cabs and beat-up trucks with graffiti-painted sides maneuver for any advantage of passing the car or truck in front of them. The streets only create the frame for the main event, which is the hundreds and hundreds of people on the sidewalks. It is a living, flowing river of heavy-coated, serious-faced strangers. Even those walking together do not talk, as the job of moving along consumes their concentrated efforts. Each person has a place to go—to work that is waiting for them to begin.

We stand like a small island in the middle of this river, luggage at our feet and dressed for the elegant promenade. We are a foreign island. My brown wool coat with a large silver fox collar extends below my shoulders. My brown hair is tucked into my hat. Charlie thinks I look like an American movie star, but I just I hope it will allow me to shield my eyes. Charlie stands tall in his dark brown camel coat and expensive shoes. I think his full, thick hair gives him the look of a dark and handsome leading man. But we do not have the script, and we do not speak the language. We have no place to go. We stand awkwardly, waiting. I use my hat to hide my anxiety. Charlie stands boldly with a wide stance and his hands behind his back, trusting the doctor will arrive momentarily.

Out of the corner of my eye, I see two bodies wrapped in blankets. They are stretched out on metal grates from which occasional feathers of steam rise. *Are they dead?* People walk by them without any alarm or concern. *Do people just walk around dead bodies in New York?* Then one of the bodies rolls over and brings his knees up to his chest. The movement is slow, but it startles me. They are sleeping! Why do people sleep on the street in such a city? I am stunned. Everything seems strange and off-kilter. Professionally-dressed women are wearing tennis shoes and carrying shopping bags. People bump into me, and then they grumble at me! It is all so strange.

"Flori and Charlie!"

The young doctor arrives, and we hug in familiar Romanian fashion, with two quick kisses on each cheek. Then he sees the bags at our feet. His face shows his alarmed surprise. "What? What have you done? Why do you have your luggage?"

"We want to stay and talk to you." Charlie smiles and greets him with another huge hug and a bigger smile. "It is all so good. I am so happy we can talk now!"

Doctor Virgil says, "Okay, there is a coffee shop right here. We will go in, and we can talk."

"Yes, yes. Let us do that. But I want to stay and talk with you."

Doctor Virgil clearly is upset about our change in plans. I realize that we are imposing on someone who doesn't know us. I am embarrassed that Charlie, an astute businessman, is just acting so happy in a child-like manner. He, who is so clever at reading people's body language and establishing the perfectly-balanced professional relationship, is now unaware of the awkwardness of this unexpected development on the street corner.

Soon we get a booth by the window and are sipping black coffee from thick white mugs, and Doctor Virgil quickly understands that Charlie wants more than a conversation over coffee. He wants to spend extended time with him in New York.

"I have so much I want to talk about," Charlie explains.

Again, I am confused. What "so much" does Charlie need to talk to him about? We are on vacation to see interesting places and things. What is it my husband needs to know?

"Yes, but tomorrow my final comprehensive medical exams begin! I must take them and pass them on the first attempt. They are comprehensive. I do not have time to spend with you today or tonight. What have you done? How can you meet up with the tour again?"

"The guide said there would not be a way. He said they would not be able to come back this way to pick us up. They are going to Cleveland and then to Washington, DC," Charlie admits.

"Do you have their number?" the doctor asked.

"No, I do not have their number."

"Where did you stay last night?"

Charlie still does not seem upset and simply says, "I don't know where the house was. It was in a neighborhood. We don't have the address."

"What did you plan?"

I lean in to hear what Charlie will answer, for I am not aware of any plan.

"I wanted to talk to you. I don't have a plan after that. I am just so happy to meet with you."

"Where will I put you? What have you done?" the doctor asked, looking up at the ceiling. Kindly, he continued and said, "What will I do with you?"

Falling back against the booth seat, I glance at the cold cup of coffee with its well-worn and slightly bent spoon. I look for a waitress to replace it, give up, and use it to stir the cream. I am so far from home, too far from Marius's morning hugs and kisses. The window next to us is steamed up, and the people rushing by outside look like an abstract painting of brown, black, and gray.

What have we done? I wonder.

"I need to study. I will take you back to my apartment on Long Island. Monk Argatu and my mother are there. It is small, and there are no extra beds, but we will try to find someone who can take you in. We have many contacts," Dr. Virgil said.

"That is good!" Charlie claps his hands and smiles as though all the problems of the world had been solved over a cup of coffee on a Manhattan corner. "We will go with you."

RAISED!

The streets are still crowded with busy people. For the first time, I look up and see the towering stone buildings with countless windows. The winter sky's overcast is reflected in hundreds of windows, perfectly matching the buildings' facades. Within steps, the doctor leads us down into the mouth of a loud, rumbling beast. The subway lights flicker, and the car bumps and sways during the thirty-minute ride to the doctor's apartment. I am smaller and farther away from my baby each hour, and countless, unknown obstacles obscure our return and reunion from my imagination.

CHAPTER 47

New York City, New York
December 3, 1991, morning
Charlie

I CANNOT BELIEVE OUR GOOD fortune to meet such a man as this young doctor. I know Flori doesn't understand, but I felt from the beginning something wonderful is going to happen on our trip. I have anticipated it with the joy of a child. I plan to follow what comes, and I am confident I will find it, or it will find me. The walk from the subway stop to the apartment takes just minutes. And soon the door is open. The warmth of the surprised Romanian greetings and customary introductions is fantastic. To be welcomed as family so sincerely by strangers fills me with excitement.

The apartment is filled with guests, who have come hoping to talk to Monk Argatu. Half a dozen people are sitting in folding chairs around the walls of the living room. Each of them is anxious to greet us and see if we have friends or places in common. Everywhere familiar words and conversations swirl, connecting us intimately. I wonder if my heart has ever felt more at home.

The people are interesting, and I ask many questions. Each is happy to retell the way in which they had met this kind priest and how well things have worked out for them.

I am curious because I have never met people like this. My friends and family have never made such drastic changes in their lives. I am astonished that someone could change everything. "How did you find work?" and "How did you learn English and find an apartment?"

Some of them immigrated years ago, and later they express interest in our thoughts about the December 1989 demonstrations that had led to the execution of President Nicolae and First Lady Elena Ceausescu. Or they ask questions about my opinions on the disappointments of the evolving new government. Mistrust lingers after a violent revolution. I am anxious to avoid all political topics with strangers, but there are many other things to share and to speak about with new Romanian friends.

The small crowd consists of people blessed by Monk Argatu's special ability to help people leave Communist Romania or who have received reward after his prayers for a critical situation. Donations are given freely without solicitation. Quickly, I relax in the warm and trusting atmosphere.

"For what are you asking so many questions?" Flori asks me as we share a few minutes on the front stoop. "What do you want to do? Stay here? What do you want to stay here for? We have nice restaurants, clean subways, and a beautiful apartment much larger than this one. What do you see that you want?" Looking in Flori's eyes I hear her silent question, "What do you want more than your son?"

I am surprised by her critical emotions. I shrug. I don't see things that are better than what we have at home. We are silent for a moment, and a taxi drops off more guests who rush up the stairs. Once we are alone again, I answer quietly, "I don't know what I want. I just am so happy. I have never been happier than since I stepped into the United States. I cannot believe I am so happy. I guess you could say I want to be this happy."

"I cannot be happy without Marius."

I reach for her hand. "I want Marius to be happy like this."

Flori does not grab my hand. "Marius will be happy when he is with his daddy and his mommy."

I nod my head. "This is true, and it is true for me too. I want to be happy together."

CHAPTER 48

New York City, New York
December 3, 1991

THE YOUNG DOCTOR MADE SEVERAL phone calls to wealthy friends with large apartments and extra bedrooms. The Madas were reassured that once these families arrived home from work in the evening, they would return the doctor's phone messages and a place would be offered. The young man retreated to his bedroom to continue his preparation for the exams.

By late afternoon, no one had returned his call. So the monk began to make calls also. "Many people come and thank me. They say if I ever need help, they will be there to help. So someone will return my calls."

As the doctor's mother began to call her friends, darkness filled the three large windows looking over the crowded and tree-lined streets. Guests continued to knock on the door to leave offerings of Romanian cakes or loaves of bread for the monk. And with each, Monk Argatu would find a quiet space in the hallway and pray a special prayer or blessing. Flori and Charlie had sought his blessings during the yearning years when they so desired to begin a family, and now they understood they were part of this great collection of individuals who admired their new friend. He was certainly beloved for his kind and gentle spirit.

Soon more guests began to arrive with large dishes that smelled like home. Coats were hung on hooks in the hallway, piling up on top of one another until it was difficult to open the door. Folding tables were quickly arranged between the living room and the kitchen, and an odd assortment of chairs and benches provided seating. The doctor, motivated by hunger or the disruption of the noise and commotion, came out of his bedroom. Dishes of steaming food were placed in the middle of the tables.

Suddenly, the room became silent. Monk Argatu offered prayers. The prayers were not the formal chanting of prayers Flori and Charlie expected. Instead, they were respectful and yet personal and specific. Monk Argatu mentioned the abundant food, the joy of Charlie and Flori's presence, and the kind hospitality of their host. Flori was speechless that the group was thanking God for their unexpected visit. The monk had mentioned, "There was little room in the inn, but Jesus himself understood the enormous blessing even humble sharing brings forth." Flori forced a smile for the first time that day.

The conversation around the table helped to inform the Madas about the nature of the elderly monk's relationship with the young doctor. Monk Argatu had paid for the young man's airline ticket, arranged for him to be able to leave Romania, and helped introduce him to trustworthy contacts. Monk Argatu had done this for many people in the New York area, and they and the family members who had later emigrated honored him. Now he was raising money to build a Romanian Orthodox Monastery near Jerusalem. Blessings and communions were expected to continue throughout the week. The monk's serious illness had been a source of enormous concern, and now they wanted to see him and celebrate his divine healing.

Charlie enjoyed the peace settling around this table. Monk Argatu was elderly and frail. He briefly shared about being poisoned while he was in the monastery. Afraid of a second attempt if he went to a hospital, he had remained in his room critically ill for three days. Several women cared and prayed for him, and on the third day, God healed him.

Others in the room discussed various other times when dissidents were rumored to have been poisoned by factions of the government. The Madas believed this to be true, and they marveled that now he was able to eat enthusiastically with the few teeth he had not lost, smiling and enjoying the conversations. Good people surrounded them, and they could not help but feel the warmth of the fellowship.

Once the dinner dishes had been cleared from the table and the folding table placed back into the closet, the guests left with promises of returning soon. The young doctor continued to make several calls, but the hour was late. It was obvious Flori and Charlie needed a place to sleep.

"Our honored Monk will sleep in my room, and I will sleep on the floor. Charlie and Flori will sleep on the couch, and my mother on the folding bed in the living room." And so on the night before his comprehensive exams, the young doctor rolled out some blankets and slept on the bedroom floor. Charlie looked not only at the sacrifice he was offering, but also at the calm, pleasant attitude in which it was offered. Had he ever met anyone like this before?

CHAPTER 49

New York City, New York
December 4, 1991

BEFORE SUNRISE, DR. VIRGIL WAS up and showered. Flori and Charlie could hear his preparation. Charlie went to the bedroom door and opened it to go out and wish him good luck. The young man was fully dressed in a professional suit and was stretched out on the floor face down, praying in the formal Orthodox manner. Charlie was overwhelmed with curiosity. Why would a successful man, fully dressed, pray in such a manner? Charlie marveled that someone who was preparing to be a doctor, not a priest, would behave in such a reverent way and take the time before exams to pray so purely.

He softly closed the door and returned to the couch where Flori was beginning to wake. They talked about the developments or lack of developments to arrange housing. "He has honored us. I am so moved and humbled," Charlie sighed. "If we do not find housing today, then I will call the number this man gave to me on the plane."

"What number, Charlie?" Flori asked.

"Oh, when I was stretching in the plane's aisle, a man started talking to me. I told him we were going to Washington, and he said he knew people who lived there. And he wrote this number down and gave it to me. I didn't even ask! He said these people liked to help other Romanians in the United States. But I like these people. I would like to stay here with them and ask them questions if we can. Let's see how the day goes."

Flori closed her eyes and wondered what Marius would be doing at this moment. She tried to see his eyes, face, and little legs learning to walk more confidently. But she could not bear to bring out the photograph she carried. She took a deep breath and tried to find the strength to face all the unknown questions and possibilities of this new, unexpected day. In several days, she would be on a plane returning to their home. They just had to find their way to Washington.

The day was overcast and cold, but early in the morning, people started arriving to spend time with Monk Argatu. If there was a break in the visitations, Monk Argatu continued to make calls to his friends, looking for accommodations for the Madas. "I cannot imagine why no one has called us back. This is difficult to understand. But God has his plan." The monk smiled his toothless grin.

The apartment was very warm, and Flori began to feel the crush in her chest. As each new hour offered no place to stay, she had an increased understanding of the burden they would be for another night. She sat and smiled, acting like she was following the continuous conversations that flowed into the small living room, but silently her private conversation was entirely different. Flori was beginning to see Charlie had little interest in making arrangements to return to Romania. She was going through different scenarios that might work out. She planned one for staying an extra week or an extra month. But the one she liked the best was an immediate return, because they were unable to find accommodations now. To Flori, no room, limited money, and few options meant it was time to go home to Romania. There seemed no time or place to be alone. She was not able to have any private conversation with Charlie, which she desperately wanted.

By the afternoon, Flori had developed a dreadful headache. Her mental examination of their situation and her observation of Charlie's strange behavior continued to be a crushing burden. Charlie was happy and smiled all the time. His child-like demeanor was uncharacteristic. He asked dozens of questions when usually he was the one answering others' questions. Charlie was educated and informed. Important people with worldly experiences enjoyed taking road lessons from him because he was an excellent teacher and an easy and interesting conversationalist. He was usually the leader in conversations, not the listener. But here he was sitting and finding everything and everyone interesting—everyone but his wife. Flori felt left behind.

The monk and the doctor's mother continued to make phone calls, but no return calls rang. Flori watched the dialing, and she monitored looks between the mother and the monk. They would look at the clock or their watches and then share a small shrug of surprise. Then they returned to their tasks of hospitality, blessings, and preparing more food.

Charlie was concentrating on everyone else but Flori, and by late afternoon her headache and her anxiety had increased. She was concerned that Charlie would not ever want to return. "I am so happy here. I have never felt anything like this. I feel like I have been living in a dry riverbed, and now sweet clean water is gently flowing. I am floating, and I feel like this is where I was always meant to be … just going with the current. It is like a dream, but I do not wake up. I continue to feel blissful and peaceful beyond anything else. I do not ever want to leave here."

Flori blinked. *There, he had said it.* This crowded apartment where they did not belong meant more to Charlie than everything— everything they had built and created at home. It was better here than with their son. He wanted to stay with these people, talk to these people. Had he even seen her today? Had his eyes rested on her and looked into her eyes and seen her distress and confusion? Had he held her hand or touched her arm? Had he thought of Marius? His business? Their families? Flori thought her head would explode. *He doesn't need to talk to me, discuss with me, and decide with me. He won't go back.*

And she suddenly felt unexpected clarity and strength. *I will stay with Charlie and not be in control. I need to allow him to go his way without understanding him. I will just observe. I can decide later what I will do. For now, I need to see and watch what he does and see how this goes. If I leave now, I may never see him again or understand what happens. But maybe he is headed for a breakdown. And he will need me.* Flori went into the bedroom and fell asleep.

Charlie watched the continued effort to find them a room, but even in the absence of secure plans, he still was experiencing a new peace. He wasn't alarmed that these powerful and influential people were not able to find one room for a night. He was relaxed.

For dinner, the doctor's mother began to prepare eggplant. It was her son's favorite, and she wanted to prepare a special dinner after his first day of exams.

"I really do not like eggplant," the monk quietly told Charlie.

"Then you do not need to eat it. She is preparing it for her son. She will understand."

The Monk shook his head slowly. "No, I will try it. If you do not try it, you might offend her. She is proud to offer this special dish to us. I will try it."

"Then I will too," Charlie vowed. He looked at the old man's face. *He is taking time to teach me to be kind. Who does that? He is teaching me that I should adjust my desire and actions in light of an old woman's feelings. He is teaching me intentionally to consider others first.* Peaceful warmth flowed from Charlie's chest throughout his body. *This is different. I am not annoyed by his instruction. I am grateful for his wisdom.* Charlie looked over at the old woman slicing thin circles of eggplant and smiled.

The doctor had not returned from his exams when Flori joined the small group to eat. They all served generous helpings to create a full plate for the young doctor when he returned. Other friends began arriving for an evening visit with the Monk Argatu in the living room. The mother finished the dishes and joined the guests.

After dinner, Charlie sat with Flori in the kitchen. "They have spent so much time on the phone trying to help us. They have been kind. I do not want to take advantage of them, Flori." Charlie took out the phone number from the plane. Flori was relieved. Washington was where the tour was headed after the visit to Cleveland. Perhaps they could rejoin the group and return on schedule.

"Yes, Charlie, you are right. I think we should call them." And so he reached over and took the black phone from the wall. The old cord was tangled like a braid, but the buttons put through the call immediately. A woman's voice answered with a familiar Romanian greeting. Charlie smiled.

Charlie spoke in Romanian, explaining they were in New York City without a place to stay. He winked and said they were staying in an apartment with Monk Argatu, hoping that information would help ease any misgivings these people might have in offering strangers help. Charlie said they were hoping to stay for a short time in Washington. They had been with a tour group, and perhaps they would rejoin the tour. They would see how things worked out.

"Yes, you should come here. We have a big house and plenty of food. We are Baptist, and we can help you stay for a while. You can stay for a bit longer. But you will need to get here to Seattle, Washington. Can you do that?"

Charlie said, "Can we get a train?"

"No, you will need to buy airline tickets."

"We can do that. The monk and doctor will help us to do that, and we have money."

"Good, let us know when you will be arriving, and I will pick you up at the airport."

Charlie hung up the phone. They each took a deep breath. They had found a place. "I don't really want to leave here. They have been so kind. But they have much to do, and I am worried they will feel too sad that they cannot find a place for us. I don't want them to feel embarrassed."

Flori reached across the table and touched Charlie's hand. "Why do we need to take a plane, Charlie? The tour was driving. Why could we not take a bus or train?"

"We will do what they say. They know; we do not."

When the doctor's mother returned, Charlie and Flori explained their new plans. She smiled broadly, and the Madas knew she was pleased they would not be staying indefinitely in the small apartment. "Seattle, Washington? I have a map. Let's see how close that is to the capital city." So she unfolded a large paper map out on the table. The three of them started searching for Seattle near Washington.

"Maybe it is such a small town. It is too small to be on this map," Flori said.

They kept looking.

"Oh wait, I think my son was offered an opportunity to work in Seattle, Washington. It was on the west coast, where it rains a lot. Maybe it is that Washington."

Flori and Charlie looked at each other. They quickly located a Seattle, Washington. But they also found numerous cities named Columbus. It was confusing that states used so many of the same names for cities. The soft cover book had a page for each state, and they finally found Seattle, Washington. However, the book did not show them where the state of Washington was in relationship to the capitol city of Washington.

"They are probably close, Flori." Charlie closed the atlas.

The couple joined the conversation in the living room. Most of the people thought Seattle, Washington was being spelled incorrectly, thus difficult to find on the map. Someone else thought it was on the West Coast, north of California. Flori and Charlie were not sure how far away California or the state of Washington was from the city of Washington. However, they all agreed that it was confusing.

"Well, we will go to Washington! Seattle, Washington." Charlie had decided. He was determined to go. An older man with a white beard who was sitting in the corner shared that Baptists were Protestants. He spoke with his eyes closed, "Well, be careful of the Protestants. They will try to take advantage of you. They will try to convert you, but they will take advantage. They are tricky." Silence punctuated the seriousness of the warning.

Monk Argatu smiled and looked directly into Charlie's eyes. "This may be true. You will need to be careful. You need to go with God and know he loves you. That is all you need to remember." And the Monk took his hand and brought it to Charlie's chest. "God loves you so much more than you can understand."

Charlie said, "Yes, I will remember this because you have told me."

"No, Charlie, remember this because Jesus tells us." The monk smiled.

"Okay, Jesus tells me." But Charlie asked himself, "How does this Jesus tell me? He is a man who died a long time ago."

"We will go with confidence." Charlie smiled.

Monk Argatu gave them a blessing and prayed the arrangements would be made as God provided. Suddenly, Dr. Virgil walked through the door, exhausted. He listened to the plan and shook his head when told not one contact had even returned their call. "Okay, then I will draw you maps to sightsee in Manhattan tomorrow. While you are there, you can exchange your tickets back to Romania and buy new ones to Seattle, Washington. I have exams during the next two days. I will do the best I can for you. Now, I need to review and then get some sleep."

The guests said goodnight, and all the apartment dwellers, respecting the young man's critical need for quiet and rest, began to retire. Charlie was happy and peaceful and quickly fell asleep. But Flori tossed and turned. And then she lay absolutely still. She did not fall asleep. This was a crazy plan. She worried they would be unable to rejoin the tour and go home. The pressure in her chest was impossible to ignore. Sleep was as far away as wherever Seattle, Washington, really was. Her only hope was that these people in Washington would change their minds or that all the details necessary for their travel would fall apart. If nothing worked, then Charlie might agree to return to Romania.

She thought of countless, different ways they might be able to all be together. She knew together was far more important than where. She knew reunion with Marius would remain her goal—together. But the stress and sadness did not depart with the sound of the early morning garbage trucks nor with the winter orange sunrise glowing on the frosted streets.

CHAPTER 50

New York City, New York
December 5, 1991

CHARLIE WOKE UP AND MET the doctor at the kitchen table before he had to leave for the second day of exams. The man's genuine interest and generosity continued to impress Charlie, and he wished they could spend more time together. However, after a quick review of the location of the tour company's New York office and the key subway stations, the young man needed to leave to get to the testing site.

The Madas gathered their papers and return tickets and headed off for a day of business transactions and general sightseeing. The morning rush of traffic and people was very much the same as two days ago. Even getting off the subway at the correct station was not an easy accomplishment, since their ability to read English was no more than matching letters with the doctor's notes and maps. But they were able to walk the block and a half and find a storefront window with the sign of the travel agency representing their tour group.

"We need to change the date of our return trip," Flori explained to the young woman behind the counter. The representative smiled and said, "Let me get you a service manager."

And that was the last smile they saw during the next fifteen minutes as they tried to exchange the ticket. No one would say anything other than the ticket was only good for the flight as listed. There was no monetary value for exchange or return. They were also told the tour company would not return any of their money for not participating in the tour to Cleveland nor would they assist them to meet the tour in Washington. Since they had volunteered to leave the tour, the total investment was non- refundable.

Charlie and Flori continued to try to get a more flexible arrangement or talk to someone else at the tour agency. Flori even suggested they just be given additional information to rejoin the group. Flori began to feel tears burn in her eyes. The people who spoke her language showed no interest or kindness. At home, people extended extraordinary effort if for no better reason than having someone owe you a favor. Flori tearfully started to explain they had a baby at home. No one smiled or offered any sympathy. They shook their heads and shuffled papers.

Finally, they asked Flori and Charlie to leave. There was nothing the office could do for them without their participation in the tour as originally planned. As the older man marched them to the door, he pointed out a nearby Delta Airline office and closed the door behind them.

Charlie was both angry and confused. "They cheated us. No one explained this was the way we would be treated here. Where is all that Romanian hospitality the brochures promised? The tour's saleslady said it would be like staying with our extended family while seeing North America. I don't understand. Why would the Romanians in America treat us like that? We are also Romanian! They took our money and gave us little for all they took."

Flori saw a dark abyss. She had touched those tickets a dozen times, just to feel the way home to Marius. Without refunds, now they might not even have enough money to buy tickets home. She knew the Romanian Airlines were booked months before the date of the flights. They might be less costly, but they were also difficult to acquire. International airlines were considerably more expensive.

"We cannot continue to impose on Monk Argatu and the doctor. We must go to Washington and have a place to stay. The people there seemed friendly, with a big house and plenty of food. I need to go and see them."

"Look, Charlie, there is the Delta Airlines office. Let's go there and see what we can do."

Inside the bright blue and white large storefront, young women in airline uniforms sat at half a dozen desks, looking very professional and eager to answer any of the Madas' questions. None of them spoke Romanian. Charlie and Flori knew three words: yes, no, tomorrow. Charlie pointed to the paper with Seattle, Washington, written carefully, and then he pointed to his calendar and the date of December 6th, the next day. "Tomorrow?" He smiled and held up two fingers.

The woman spoke English slowly and rather loudly. She continued even though neither Charlie nor Flori understood a word she was saying. She finished, ending with what probably was a question since her voice went higher at the end. Charlie and Flori shrugged their shoulders, smiled and then laughed. Flori said in Romanian, "We do not understand English. We need to buy two tickets to Seattle, Washington, tomorrow. How much will that be?"

Then to Flori's complete shock, the woman answered her in English, but Flori understood it. She didn't hear the Romanian words; she heard the English words, and she understood.

"You do not have enough money to go there. You need to try United Airlines. They have cheaper flights." Flori looked at her. How had she been able to understand the English? How had the woman been able to understand her Romanian? And how did the woman know they did not have enough money? Neither Flori nor Charlie had indicated how much money they carried. And in a blink, the woman continued to speak in English as foreign and incomprehensible as it had always been. And Flori understood nothing but the few times the word "United" was used. The pointing down the street and turning right was in the international language of hand signals. So they left the Delta Airlines office and found themselves on the street.

"Charlie, did you understand her when she told us we did not have enough money and we should try United Airlines? How did she know how much money we have?"

Charlie looked at her, "How did you understand her? She only spoke English."

"I don't know, but I did. And then I couldn't again. Did you understand the directions to the United Airlines office?"

"No, I thought you understood them the way you were nodding your head."

Flori laughed and buttoned the top button of her coat. "I do not understand how I understood everything she was saying. And then I understood nothing."

The pressure of the river of people on the sidewalks began to push them along. They walked with the crowd toward the closest corner and then across a wide, busy street. And they continued to walk down another block to avoid the bumping and pushing of the hundreds of New Yorkers going to work.

"How will we find the United office?" Flori asked Charlie. He looked down at her without an answer.

"Let's take a right turn at the next corner and perhaps we can find a place in the doorway to avoid all the pushing."

Flori edged her way toward the buildings on the right side of the sidewalk. As soon as she got to the corner, she turned right and walked two-dozen steps along the street to the first doorway. Charlie was following right along behind her.

"Now what?" Flori looked up at Charlie and then began to laugh. "Look!" And she pointed behind his head to the large United Airlines sign and a huge, blue and white airplane model hanging in the window. They had unknowingly been pushed by the crowd from the Delta Airlines office east two blocks, across a wide and busy street, and then had turned at the exact spot of the United Airlines office door.

"How could this be?" Charlie laughed, and they both pushed through the turning doors and into yet a third travel office.

The Madas used the American cash they still had in their bags to purchase two, one-way tickets to Seattle, Washington. Flori hated to spend over nine hundred dollars to travel farther away from Marius, but Charlie was obsessed with meeting these people and talking to them.

"Why come this far and then leave with such a yearning to understand more? When will we ever return to have this opportunity again?"

"But Charlie, we don't have enough cash even to buy tickets to return to New York, much less Romania," Flori said. She continued to suppress her growing uneasiness that Charlie's unprecedented happiness was seducing him into thinking about staying. In her mind, she hoped the more he scratched the itch, the sooner he would want to return to their settled lives in Romania. He would have many interesting, new stories to tell friends and driving students. Things would go back to normal. He would start acting like himself. She loved him, and they had been through so much. If she had to wire their parents to liquidate some of their property, it could be done. They were not without resources. For now, she needed to let Charlie just do what he needed to do and go where the river flowed. They would get back to normal again. She believed that was true. After paying the United representative, Flori counted out the remaining eighty dollars and placed this money next to the tickets in the zippered pocket of her bag.

With the tickets purchased and safely in Flori's handbag, the couple was free to enjoy the rest of the day in the city. They wandered around the financial district and Twin Towers. In the glass-walled lobby, people were dressed much more like what the Madas would expect from professionals. Although the women wearing sneakers and business suits seemed odd, Flori looked down at her high heels. The black shoes were elegant, and she was happy she had them on. Walking as quickly as these American women would have been impossible, but she was in no hurry. But these people were preoccupied with the places and people they needed to see. The people all filed into large elevators and disappeared up into their careers. Flori and Charlie both felt invisible, overwhelmed by the size and energy of the city.

They decided to head uptown to see Times Square, Fifth Avenue stores, and all the way up to Rockefeller Center. They took their time walking around the huge Christmas tree. Leaning over the railing, they watched skaters of various skills twirl and fall on the ice rink below. Christmas energy filled Rockefeller Center, and the windows in the department stores were sparkly and elegant. Charlie was exhaustively excited, and Flori was equally disengaged. They were leaving the next day, headed away from Marius and home. Flori had chosen the middle road. She was not thinking too much about happy or terrifying things. She smiled when Charlie smiled; she laughed when he laughed. She made great small talk. She was there, and she wasn't. Charlie was so happy he didn't notice.

The lights began to come on around 4:15 in the afternoon as the early winter sunset and low clouds brought an end to the daylight. Surrounded by the red brake lights of taxis and the green traffic lights of Fifth Avenue, the city became much more festive. They would have enjoyed staying longer. However, they headed back to the train station, and they were back at the apartment by the polite hour of nine with all of their eighty dollars and growling stomachs.

The doctor quickly answered the front door, making the sign of the cross. "Oh, thank God. I thought I would never see you again." He grabbed each in a big hug as they entered the apartment.

"We have the tickets for a flight tomorrow morning. We will pack and be on our way tomorrow. Thank you so much for all your hospitality. We are sorry we have added extra stress during your testing." Flori immediately saw the doctor and his mother were both surprised and quietly relieved. As unexpected guests, they were a welcomed blessing, but the apartment was small. It would be easier to have fewer people in the apartment.

Monk Argatu prayed for them sincerely. Ever since he had heard the story about Marius on the flight from Romania, he marveled at their blessing. Many of his meetings with supporters involved personal situations, so they met in private. But later in a small group, Monk Argatu would announce Charlie and Flori had a compelling story, and Charlie and Flori would share a short version of Marius's miracle. It had extended many visits and conversations. He would miss the Madas. He marveled at the blessing these two, young people had experienced. And surely God had anointed them for a great purpose. How could the story be true and that not be true also?

But he could see Charlie and Flori seemed very naive spiritually. They were pilgrims, unaware of the journey's destination. It would be exciting to be with them when they understood what God had done for them. But he was old, and he had been blessed to be at the harvest many times during his lifetime. To still be useful in the preparation of such spiritual soil was a humbling honor in itself.

His prayer for their safety and journey was simple and loving, and it touched the Madas' hearts. As he put his bearded face down on the couch's pillow, he instantly fell asleep, dreaming of wonderfully rich, green vineyards and wooden wagons overflowing with large, purple grapes. The workers sang a song, but he couldn't quite hear the words yet. It was one of his favorite dreams.

For the third night, Dr. Virgil slept on the floor. And everyone was up early the next morning saying how nice it was to meet, promising to keep in touch, and checking and double-checking the tickets and bags.

As Dr. Virgil pulled up next to the Kennedy Airport curb, he got out to give Charlie a final hug. Reaching into his pocket, he pulled out one hundred dollars and offered it to Charlie. "Here, you will need this. Call me to let me know where you are. And come back when our situations are different. I cannot believe Monk Argatu and I could not find you a room to stay."

Charlie hesitated to take the money, as it was clear the doctor and his mother did not have a lot of money. He was afraid he would insult him like refusing eggplant might insult his generous hostess. He thanked him and promised to stay in touch. Waving goodbye to the small car's back window, Charlie wondered if he would ever meet such gentle and kind people again. Then he turned to Flori and said, "I am so excited to go and meet these new people. It is just so wonderful."

Flori smiled back. "Yes, Charlie, it is very exciting." Parroting didn't require too much thought or conviction.

CHAPTER 51

Not Washington, DC—the State of Washington
Friday, December 6, 1991
Charlie

THE DIRECT FLIGHT FROM NEW York to Seattle took off before sunrise, so I can catch up on sleep. Next to me Flori is counting our money. Each time it is exactly $180.00. Flori stayed up late last night to write a letter to Aunt Cristina and short notes to our parents, explaining we are going to Seattle, Washington, to visit Romanian people we had met through friends on the plane. The letters had sounded ridiculous to Flori, and she describes to me how she imagines them opening the letters and reading these mysterious words. Certainly, this will not make any sense to them. Each family will sit after dinner in their own homes, drinking a glass of wine or beer, and they will speculate about what is happening and how it could explain these developments.

Flori explains that Aunt Cristina will need to change her plans and stay longer at our apartment. I don't know if that will be a problem for her. Flori insists no possible explanation will satisfy them or prevent confusion and worry. I don't know if Flori's imagination and worry are true. I think we should wait to hear directly from them, what their reaction will be, and then we can deal with them. So I had told her to keep the letters short, and she had.

As the hours stretch on, Flori finally falls asleep for short periods of time. I know she is worried about how many miles the plane has traveled during the long trip. She sighs, asks how many kilometers per hour the plane's travels, and looks at her watch. I know she is calculating miles of empty land passing below her small plane window. It is true that it is longer and farther than I expected.

The plane finally lands at noon under Seattle's gray skies. The airport is much smaller than Kennedy Airport, so we easily retrieve our bags and manage to find the atrium. I find a pay phone and pull the same slip of paper from the Romanian flight out of my coat pocket. Flori stands close with the two leather bags and two small duffle bags at her feet.

She also hears the deep, Romanian voice booming over the phone line. "Yes, yes, we were expecting to hear from you. Excuse my voice, as I am ill with a cold. My wife is at work, but we have members of our church who will pick you up on their way down to Friday night services."

"You will not pick us up?" I am disappointed.

"No, you are far away from where we live. I am too ill, and this family has offered. They live in Tacoma, and they will drive right by the airport. They will bring you to us when they come to services tonight. They will come inside the terminal and find you by the main door. Be ready for them at five o'clock."

Four-hours go by quickly as we watch the people come and go. These people are dressed even more casually than those in New York, some even in jeans with flannel shirts. There is even a man wearing a cowboy hat like in the few Wild West movies we have seen. Adidas sneakers in lots of different colors seem to be the favorite footwear of young people.

Flori is wearing her best dress and high heels with her silver fox collared coat. I am again wearing my dark brown camel overcoat. We laugh and tease each other that we will be easy to recognize as Romanian even in the hustle and bustle of the crowded terminal.

"Bine ati venit in Seattle!" Shortly after five o'clock, a Romanian greeting is called out across the terminal hall. A man is smiling and waving, and a woman who looks to be his wife hurries across the hall. Following them is an older couple carrying a newborn baby.

"Charlie and Flori Mada! Welcome to Seattle! What a long day you have had. I am Tudor, and this is my wife, Ligia. And my parents and our son." The genuine warmth of the greetings comforts the aches of a very long day sitting in an airplane and on the hard seats of the airport. Hugs and Romanian cheek kisses are all exchanged. After watching dozens and dozens of families reunite at the airport, this enthusiastic welcome has a warming effect on me.

"Welcome! Here, let me help with the bags." Tudor picks up one and his father another, and we are soon headed to the parking lot to find the family's white minivan. By five o'clock the sun has set, and the ride gives us little view of the community. We have a lively conversation about jobs and families. The family seems truly happy and excited about our visit.

CHAPTER 52

Not Washington, DC—the State of Washington
Friday, December 6–7, 1991
Flori

THE FORTY-MINUTE DRIVE GOES BY quickly, and soon we pull into a dimly lit parking lot.

I know it is not at the church. The two brick buildings could be office buildings, but not a church. The Byzantine architecture and soaring domes that distinguish a church are missing.

"Why have we stopped here?" I whisper. I am apprehensive and do not want to get out. My question is ignored as the family piles out and begins greeting others who approach our car. My mind recalls memories of dinner conversations in Romania about wild stories of the unpredictable behavior by Protestants. "Do we really know these people enough to trust them with our lives? The people in New York warned us about Protestants. What have we done? We are here in this parking lot, and we have few options."

If Charlie has any similar concerns, he does not express them, as he quickly gets out of the car and begins introducing himself. I just sit inside the open car door.

A thin man wearing a suit jacket approaches us and with a very deep, husky voice and says, "Welcome, Charlie Mada! I am Pastor Doru, and this is my wife, Vio." The youthfulness of the man startles me. I carefully watch Charlie. He smiles and nods, and we both continue to search the crowd for the bearded face of the priest.

"For whom are you looking? Charlie, I told you I am the pastor. I spoke with you."

"You are the priest? You do not look like a priest!" I am relieved that my husband is cautious.

Everyone laughs. Doru says, "Pastor, Charlie, not priest. In the Baptist Church, there is no priest." Vio comes to the door and takes my hand. I tentatively step out and accept her warm welcome.

I ask her, "Where is the church? This isn't a church!"

"Oh, we believe the church is in the hearts of the believers, Flori. That is where Lord Jesus builds his kingdom." Vio puts an arm around my shoulder. "You have had a long trip today. We are going to take care of you. First, we will have Bible study, and then we will get you home and feed you. We have prepared a place for you to sleep tonight."

Inside the church's music room, the small group of Romanian Christians is arranging chairs for their weekly Bible study. A large piano and folding chairs dominate the center of the room, which is unattractive and cluttered, but clean and warm. I am only comfortable because of the wonderful chatter of a dozen-and-a-half Romanians, who are all talking at once. Greetings are lengthy, and no one is rushing to begin the evening's events. The women smile and invite me into their comfortable, familiar chatter.

Shortly, Charlie pulls me aside. "Flori! Isn't this amazing? The leader is not a priest. He dresses like we do, and he doesn't have a beard! No candles, no altar, no icons to kiss. Everyone seems so happy. They are more than friends. We do not have friends who love each other as these do." Charlie gushes on about the excitement of the group's obvious joy in gathering together. "I am so glad we have come here. I didn't think anything like this existed."

I look around. He is right. There is not a beautiful sanctuary. There are no icons with gold, rich blues, and red accents on paintings of favored saints. No soft candles are flickering with the whispers of mysterious chants. Nor are there white streams of heavy incense rolling toward a vaulted, painted ceiling. Here, a drop tile ceiling hangs above folding chairs, and homemade, felt banners' appliqués curl and peel. The brown boxes of old hymnals piled in the corner are breaking down into several tilting towers. Greenish, fluorescent light washes over everyone's pale, winter complexions.

But Charlie is right. Lively, loving conversations fill the room, and smiles glow with a different kind of light. I am used to churches having an imposing distant silence which makes me want to escape. There is warmth in this room. The kind of warmth that radiates from people interacting and caring about one another, looking into each other's eyes and reacting to news—sad or happy—with expressive faces. People are not hushed in a soft candlelight, but there are warm and loud greetings for the new arrivals. Introductions fly, and immediately several families offer to let us stay in their homes. I feel less apprehension, but all of this warmth and love flows between friends. I am a stranger here, and their joy makes me feel even farther away from my home and our son.

We sit down, and Charlie whispers, "Let's just try to fit into this. It is very different from any church service I have ever attended!"

I nod in agreement. Soon the twenty or so people settled down into chairs. The men sit on the right side, and the women and children sit on the other side, and everyone carries or picks up a Bible. So we sit down in the back, across the aisle from each other and are introduced yet again. Charlie stands and expresses appreciation for the many kind invitations. He explains we will stay with the pastor tonight, but we look forward to getting to know everyone.

Within an hour and a half, we arrive at the pastor's home, enjoy a much-needed meal, and are shown our room. The pastor's study is downstairs, but the property drops off in the backyard. The family refers to it as a "walkout basement," but it doesn't feel like a basement. There are two large rooms and a bathroom. The pastor's son, Chris, uses the bedroom with a sliding glass door. The pastor's study has a large desk, two chairs for counseling, and rich, wooden shelving for his library.

The room is warm and quiet with attractive blinds and drapes. Exhausted, we fall into the pullout sofa bed. But sleep does not relieve my exhaustion, and I know Charlie is also awake reviewing all that has happened.

Charlie whispers to test if I am asleep. "When the pastor stood up, I wondered where would he sit? There was not a chair in the room that looked grand enough for the pastor to sit down in to teach."

I laugh. "I thought so too. Why do they stand to teach? Don't teachers usually sit and begin teaching? And when Pastor Doru opened a very old and worn book and began to read aloud, I was so surprised. Do you remember how grand the Bible is in the Orthodox Church? There are even precious jewels on it."

"And he didn't put it on a stand. He held the Bible! They must be ignorant. They do not know any better."

"It sounds like a modern version of the scripture. But Pastor Doru reads with so much expression. He seems to like the Holy Scripture, but it does not look like he honors the Bible. Why would he let his Bible look like such an old book? And his wife wrote in hers!"

"Why do they all have Bibles? It is the Holy Book. Only the priest should touch it." I can feel Charlie nodding his head in agreement.

"They are not respectful. They talk about God like he is a person they know. You would not call the president of the country by his first name. Why would you just call God, Jesus? It is as if no one ever taught them any better."

"Well, we were warned about them."

Charlie gives me a loving hug. "They are nice. They are happy and kind."

"It is very confusing."

"Yes, but it is more interesting than confusing. Things are different than I expected. But I am also happier than I expected. I asked John why they touched and held the Holy Bible. He explained, 'The Bible was a gift to every man and woman.' He spoke so gently to me. They explained it humbly. I asked him the question with a tone of voice that was not humble. I thought he just didn't know any better. My tone said, 'You are naive and don't know as much as I do.' But he answered me so sweetly. It made me ashamed of the way I asked the question. Flori, I have never heard anyone ask a question about what the Bible means. At home, I did not even listen when the priest read the Bible. Here, their pastor doesn't read it in a boring manner. It is almost like music. Here, they take it very seriously. They ask questions, and the pastor answers them. And others can add their opinion or insight. It is all I can think about."

"Our first group of Protestants. We know Protestants now! I was confused when I first saw them in the parking lot. It was dark; I was tired, and it didn't look like any church I have seen." I yawn and re-adjust the pillow.

"I talked to one man who is visiting here. He is working in New York City, but he wants to be here in Washington to be part of the Romanian community here. He was interesting. I want to talk to him more tomorrow."

"Still, Charlie, everything is so different. I miss our son, our home."

"Flori, I am here. I will take care of you. They seem like good people, but I am here. I will watch, and I will take care of you. Tomorrow, I will talk more to them. They have captured my interest. I want to look at the meanings of these new words. I have lots of questions about the Bible and Jesus."

This is the husband I know, and he begins to explain flaws in some of the reasoning of the pastor's answers. Charlie likes to debate, and he is preparing to challenge the group tomorrow. I am smiling in the dark.

Sometime during the early morning hours, I awake filled with resentment. Charlie is sleeping soundly next to me. Motionless and silently I wrestle with ideas. Where will we sleep tomorrow? Next week? How many weeks will it be before we can return to New York City and then fly home to Romania? How much time will Charlie need to stay? How long will it be before we leave? How much money will this family want for food and letting us sleep here? How will we get that money? Then I drift off to sleep for a few minutes, wake, and am startled and confused by the unfamiliar room. The same list of questions and uncertainties attack over and over again.

The next morning, I find the kitchen to be lively and full of the pastor's family and friends gathering around the table. The pastor holds a Bible study in his home every week, and people arrive early for small talk and breakfast. George and Claudia and their three children are like part of the family. Charlie and I laugh and enjoy new friends. Even before the second cups of coffee are poured, more people arrive.

When we are asked about our family, we share the story of Marius and all the incredible events that have brought us to this kitchen in Washington State. Pastor Doru and the others listen intently only to interrupt by saying, "Thank you, Jesus!" Others lift their arms above their heads and shout, "Praise Jesus!" The group is deeply moved by the story in a way no others have been. I look around and see that most are extremely emotional and empathetic. Claudia puts her arms around me during the worst moments of the story. Many cry during the best parts. The pastor explains his faith credits Marius's recovery and life to Jesus's divine intervention, and this faith multiplies the congregation's joy and excitement. The overflowing tears and praise take me aback. Even our own friends in Romania did not react with this much empathy for what we went through.

Pastor Doru suggests the group give thanks to God. Immediately the group quiets themselves, some kneeling. The beauty and holiness of the pastor's words touch me deeply. It is so personal as he specifically mentions events in the story and gives thanks to God. Charlie reaches out for my hand and presses it so hard that I know this outpouring of love also has sincerely moved him. The unity of praying together gives me unexpected strength and encouragement. This group believes Charlie, Marius, and I are in the hand and heart of God. I have never had such a comforting thought.

The morning study finishes with several readings about everything being possible for God. The intimacy of the morning lingers, and it doesn't seem like people want to leave. The pastor's wife is an especially gentle woman, and she brings two brown leather Bibles into the room. George takes the Bibles and writes in calligraphy "Charlie Mada" in one and "Florentina Mada" in the other. As these Bibles are given to us, someone offers a prayer that the words will be a blessing to guide our family for the rest of our lives.

A warm and intimate feeling is woven together and mixed with humble kindness and easy laughter. I begin to think this is a safe and good place to be until Charlie snaps back to himself and we can go home to our life with Marius. I look over and see Charlie's wonderful smile and easy laughter. I let a slow breath out. *I don't know why, but this is okay for a while. I just need to wait and see.*

CHAPTER 53

Not Washington, DC—the State of Washington
Saturday, December 7, 1991
Bible Study
Charlie

THE GROUP BEGINS TO GROW, and smaller groups break away and have smaller conversations. In the larger front room, I begin to speak to a man named James. I recognize in him my own interest in debate. We enjoy playful, verbal combat on a wide range of topics. We each start by asking a question to establish an important point. Other people join us and then wander away as the friendly intensity increases.

James says, "You are a successful businessman in Romania. Why are you here? What are you looking for, Charlie?"

I answer, "Yes, we are more than comfortable. We have a good life in Romania. We are lucky. But I am interested in many things. I needed to come and see."

"See what, my friend?"

"What I have not seen." I smile.

James laughs. "You are most interesting and fun to talk with, Charlie. Then let's talk about what we know and have not seen." I think that James is both clever and good.

James has switched the conversation to religion.

I challenge him. "How do we know Jesus even lived? Maybe he is just like a superhero to entertain the masses and calm the fearful."

"Then why would eleven men leave their lives and follow in paths of such suffering, imprisonment, and martyrdom for a story?

Why would hundreds of early Christian believers die at the hands of Roman circuses and not denounce Jesus Christ? Why do people count their suffering as gain, if Jesus was nothing?"

Our conversation goes on for over an hour. Most of my reasoning stems from commonly held Communist teachings that religion is the expression of old myths to explain the unknowable or unanswerable.

Then James says, "Why did they change the calendar after Jesus? Why do men and kings honor him? Who was this Jesus? If he was just a poor man who died without power or property, why is he honored in this way? Why did the calendar not change after Alexander, or Napoleon, or Edison?"

I have no answer.

"If you do not know, you will find all the answers here in the Bible." James picks up and hands me the Bible the group presented to me.

I look at him silently. I do not know enough about Jesus to answer. James has finished the conversation. I have lost to James, and I taste a bit of anger and much sadness. I bite my lip searching for any nonsense to change the subject or minimize the absence of an impressive reply. I stand there holding the Bible. "Okay, okay." I shake my head.

Immediately, James stands up and embraces me. "Brother, I like talking with you. You are a clever fellow. You know much about politics, economics, and history."

We end the evening as friends. I soon retreat to our room. I am tired, and my body feels heavy. I understand that it is because I lost to James. Tonight, I had shown that I do not have an adequate Biblical knowledge to support my opinions or even to ask challenging questions. He had an advantage, and his patience and respectful explanations had been kind. His advantage and his kindness make me uncomfortable.

After about forty minutes of tossing and turning, I turn on the light next to my bed. Flori is still upstairs chatting with other wives. I reach down next to the foldout bed and pick up the Bible. Quickly opening to the New Testament, I begin to read. I had only once before opened a Bible to read. It was years ago, and the Old Testament seemed irrelevant and did not hold my interest. My commitment lasted only a few days. My interest is different this time, because I am anxious to be prepared to participate intelligently in the conversations. I want to earn the respect of these men and to continue to be a "clever fellow" and impress James with informed points and details.

I am also curious about this big, loving God. Who was Jesus? Who does the Bible say he was? Why do these kind, generous people love Jesus so much? How does even the idea of Jesus influence their lives 2000 years later? I read late into the night, finally turning off the light when the bare branches of trees in the backyard are black silhouettes against a dark gray morning sky.

CHAPTER 54

Kirkland, Washington
Sunday, December 8, 1991

CHARLIE WOKE WITH THE SUNRISE and began hunting through the Bible again. James had mentioned a man who lived for more than 900 years, and Charlie wanted to read that for himself. A quest for something more than information had captured him, and one passage or story led to another. He read for over two hours. The search for a competitive edge had given rise to a more general and growing desire to study scripture. As Flori slept beside him, Charlie searched for evidence in the scripture to support his beliefs.

"What are you doing? Reading the Bible?" Flori stretched and held her hands over her eyes. The library was downstairs, and the drapes looked lovely, but they did not close to block the morning light.

"I am checking out what they said about God."

She laughed and said, "Oh, I see the fighting glint in your eye. Are you looking for their errors?"

"Well, yes. I don't want just to accept their word for it. If they say they believe it, then it should be in the Bible. They have very different ideas than I have ever heard before. Why do they think the way they do with such confidence?"

Flori smiled. "Oh, now I see my husband again." She was pleased to see Charlie's attitude. How many times had she seen him come home from a driving lesson and research an event or idea? Being well-read and informed had earned Charlie an excellent reputation with influential people. He knew a great deal about history and philosophy. He didn't need to believe in something to find it interesting. This desire to know about Jesus was completely consistent with his personality. This was familiar to Flori. His conversational skills had won him many recommendations. This was who he was. She enjoyed seeing the familiar and competitive part of him emerge.

For his part, Charlie did feel alive in a new and exciting way. He was thrilled to be with these people. He did want to challenge them and win their respect, but he didn't want to beat them. What if all they had told him was true? He could see something in these people he had never seen in anyone else.

"I do not understand, Flori, but I know this is the right place at the right time for us."

Charlie had not looked up from the book. Flori looked over at him before heading out of the room to the bathroom. He was intensely engaged in refuting the Protestants. This was a good start to the day.

Flori wrote to her family and another note to Aunt Cristina. There was so much still to be resolved. "Where do I begin to explain what I don't understand?" she quietly mumbled, as her pen paused above the floral notepaper Vio had given to her. She certainly didn't want to tell them Charlie was still on a quest she did not understand. She didn't want to tell them all of her fears that Charlie would just go off and disappear had been very justified. Leaving their precious Marius was unthinkable, but it had been necessary. So what else was there to say?

She wrote of this family's kindness to strangers. Vio had told Flori their home was open to the Madas, everywhere but for the master bedroom. She and Charlie could use whatever and go wherever they wished. They had a room to themselves and plenty of food. Flori said she would write a little each day and let them know their plans. She told them to kiss and hug her son and that she loved them all.

She tried not to imagine what they would say or how they would roll their eyes or talk to their neighbors about this decision. Flori avoided picturing Aunt Cristina watching Marius growing and learning new words, and taking him to the park where he would be curious about why squirrels sat on tree limbs and wiggled their tails. She knew Aunt Cristina would be sad that Flori was missing this magic—Marius's magic, which lit up the world.

Flori turned on the warm water and stepped into the shower. There no one would hear her muffled sobs or wonder why her eyes were red. She slid down the wet, tiled walls and let the longing wash over her. Before she was ready, but within the limited time of a reasonable shower, Flori pulled herself together and dried both her emotions and her body.

An hour later, after her hair and makeup were Promenade-perfect, Flori came up to the kitchen. The day was spent in typical household chores and conversations. Charlie continued to read the Bible for the next few days. The more he read, the quieter he became. He began to feel his attitude change, as he understood how Jesus interacted with all types of people. Each story showed a new aspect of Jesus's character. His friends were like people Charlie knew. Peter was impulsive but smart. How patient Jesus was to everyone!

CHAPTER 55

Kirkland, Washington
Friday, December 13, 1991
Charlie

WHEN I ENTER THE USUALLY busy kitchen, I find it empty since the Pastor and his wife have left early to go to work. The men and women of the church are hardworking individuals. Chris, the fifteen-year-old son in the family, wanders into the room and pours himself a rather large bowl of cereal. We nod a friendly greeting.

"Do you have school today?" I ask.

"Yes, the bus will pick me up." The boy shrugs his shoulders. He points to the open Bible on the table. "Are you understanding?"

Normally, I would not have admitted to a young boy that I am having trouble understanding anything. Not expecting a teenager to have the interest or the answers, I reply, "I don't understand how the God of the Old Testament and the God of the New Testament are the same. They seem like they are different."

The teenager shoves several serving spoons of breakfast into his mouth and says simply, "Without understanding the Old Testament, you cannot understand why Jesus had to come and suffer."

I expect more, but Chris keeps eating. The previous night at weekly Bible study, everyone had been talking at once. It was confusing as they all tried to explain about the need for Jesus's suffering. The words seemed like formal church talk. This morning, I am waiting for Chris to continue, but he only continues to eat. I really expect him to repeat the long explanations of the night before.

Finally, I ask, "Do you understand this book?"

"Well, I hear God's voice, and I feel Jesus's love. But I don't understand everything." Chris stops talking to take another spoon of cereal.

"I would like to understand that much—God's voice and Jesus's love. Maybe it would be a very good start." I pick up the box to see what he finds so delicious.

Chris looks up. "Do you want me to show you some stuff?"

"Okay," is my simple reply.

Chris starts showing me the presence of Jesus in all scripture by beginning in the Old Testament and working his way through Abraham, Isaiah and all the prophets. The boy uses simple language and does not give too much information or too many opinions. He never tells me what I should think or believe. He suddenly stops talking, leaving me to ask questions to finish the story.

Suddenly Chris looks up at the clock. "Whoa, I got to get to the bus stop." He picks up his backpack and runs out the door.

I am ready after school to continue the conversation. By the time dinner is served, we have made it through the Old Testament and have begun talking about Jesus. I have a hundred questions, and the boy patiently answers each by finding the passage in scripture that answers them. It almost becomes a game. There isn't a question that scripture doesn't guide us to answer.

During the evening, the conversations move from the kitchen to the living room, and then back to the kitchen again. I am astonished at how much this boy can explain with so few words and at how much he can eat! And he is calm, never waving his arms around or raising his voice.

"The connection between the Old and New Testament is the covenant. In the Old, a perfect lamb was needed to sacrifice for atonement of sins. In Jesus, God accepted a perfect lamb for all time. Jesus's perfection made any additional sacrifices unnecessary. Jesus's life was personal. He came among us and knew us and was made known to us. Therefore, our relationship with Jesus is personal. He seeks our company and companionship in a personal way rather than a group relationship as the Jewish nation enjoyed."

By the time Chris is explaining the details of the cross, I am beginning to feel weak. "I cannot understand why Jesus would hang on the cross for us when we are still so sinful and selfish."

"Well, that is understanding Jesus's love. We are unable to understand something that big. It is beyond us, but yet it has been given to us."

After midnight, I stand up and wrap Chris up in a bear hug. "Thank you."

Chris hugs me back, patting my back three times and then reaching for the half sandwich left on the plate. "Sure, anytime."

I pick up the Bible and walk down to the converted bedroom. The weakness grows. With this new understanding comes a sense of shame. I feel my past attitude of scorn for people who took the worship of Jesus so seriously. Clips of mocking words come back to sting my conscience. I was respected and rewarded in Romania for my attitude and self-confidence. I believed that I was smarter and superior to most of the people I met. Now I cringe, knowing I have been a very proud fool. The tears flow freely. Who am I to mock a God whose love was so great? God let his son choose to die to save sinful humans? This loving father, who could have saved his son, loves humans enough to accept his son's gift of life for them. I remember how much I wanted to save my innocent son. I feel the entire world tilt, and I am standing on new, unfamiliar ground.

I break down with shame and sit on the floor, leaning against the couch. When I finally can stand again, I turn the shower's faucet around to hot. The bathroom fills with steam, coating the mirror with condensation. I see the reflection of my face. Dragging my hand down the foggy glass, I uncontrollably sob. The mirror exposes my distorted face. "Oh God, what have I been? What have I done?"

Soon the shower's hot water washes over my head, overcoming my tears with cleansing waves of comfort. Motionlessly, I whisper, "If you are willing to come into such a lost and sinful heart, please come in and change me."

The warmth from the shower cannot be the source of the cool confidence that calms me. It powerfully surges through my body, filling me with joy and stopping my body-wrenching sobs. "I will call you Lord Jesus. I understand who you are. You are not only Jesus. You are my Lord."

Relaxation replaces tension. Peace throws out fear. Brotherhood wins over competitiveness. I fall asleep thinking God has prepared this place for us in Seattle, Washington. "Imagine that." I fall asleep knowing we are right where we were always meant to be, with Lord Jesus.

CHAPTER 56

Kirkland, Washington
Saturday, December 14, 1991

CHARLIE WOKE UP WITH A clear memory and awe of what had happened the night before. It was not something he had to remember; it just seemed like a part of him. "Flori, I accepted Lord Jesus last night."

Flori looked at Charlie. *What next?* she wondered. *He must be saying that to please the pastor and his family. Good, they will let us stay.*

She looked at him. "Okay." Then she turned and made the bed.

Charlie found Pastor Doru in the living room reading over his sermon notes. "I accepted Lord Jesus!" Although Pastor Doru seemed surprised, he received the news immediately. Charlie shouted as they embraced, "I feel like I had nothing. I was nothing. Now I have everything. I love everything. I love everyone! It feels like a popcorn happy."

The pastor laughed and prayed for him. "Come with me to the church tomorrow. We will tell others, and they will rejoice and pray for you too." And so the morning was filled with prayers of thanksgiving and songs of praise. And Charlie heard the words of the prayers and the lyrics of the songs as if they were a new language. He was filled with a desire to love Lord Jesus with the same thankfulness.

Over the next week, Flori watched this new behavior. She understood it as an act. *Charlie is playing along. What else could it be?* He was determined to learn all the words and melodies to the songs and all the meanings of the prayers or scripture. He was pretending to be exactly what he had so cleverly mocked in Romania—a zealous, religious man.

Flori marveled that Charlie never asked how they could reunite with Marius. He never talked about returning to their apartment, his career, or successful business. He did not ask about his family or friends. He seemed almost silly happy. She watched and didn't understand. Each day, it separated them with a widening silence. Her constant thoughts were cognitive mazes of how various paths might successfully bring her back to their home, and to their lives that revolved around the darling son whom they had almost lost. These plans coiled and tangled her thoughts, and anything interrupting them was an unwelcomed intrusion. She became very skilled at listening to conversations or Bible studies and not thinking about anything anyone else said.

Charlie never asked her what she was thinking. He was here in Washington; she was searching for a way back to everything she loved. She fantasized if she could get Marius to Washington, she could stay with Charlie until he wanted to return to their home. A few times she beat back the thought that if she just began to plan her return to Romania, maybe the shock would wake Charlie up, and he would go with her or follow her. But what would happen to him, to her, to their family if he didn't? What would happen to them if he did return against his wishes?

CHAPTER 57

Kirkland, Washington
December 15–20, 1991

WITH CHRISTMAS APPROACHING, THE WEEK passed quickly. Except for a daily walk in the neighborhood, Flori was inside most of the time. She helped with the dishes and cooking, and they made sure the home was tidy when Pastor Doru and his wife returned from their jobs. The pastor's family had a cleaning service, and on several days a week they would go to work in the evening. Occasionally, Flori and Charlie would also go and help.

The home seemed to have an open-door policy, and many friends and church members would stop by. One day, a man arrived before the pastor had returned home. Charlie began asking him questions about prayer and the Christian life.

"Why do you ask me this, Charlie?" he took another sip of the coffee Charlie had prepared and offered.

"I accepted Lord Jesus, and I want to know everything," Charlie smiled and placed a pastry from the night before in front of him.

"You do not need to say that. You do not need to change your religion. There is a Romanian Orthodox community that would give you a place to stay and food to eat."

"No, no. I found that Lord Jesus is true. I want to learn more about him. I am so happy to learn more and more."

Flori came into the room and overheard the exchange. She knew her husband's body language, and he was agitated by the conversation. He stood up and went over to the sink to get more water in his glass.

"Don't be dumb. I will find you room and food without making you a dumb, religious man." The man laughed and put his coffee mug down with a bang.

Flori stepped into the room. She had seen Charlie's temper flare with far less provocation. This man had called Charlie a dumb, religious man. She expected Charlie to grab him by the shirt and put him up against the wall. To her astonishment, he just looked at the man and calmly stated, "Learning more about Lord Jesus is the smartest thing I have ever wanted to do."

Flori looked at Charlie's face. He wasn't faking this new attitude. He was profoundly different. It didn't seem like he was overcoming his temper or controlling his anger. He was so confident in his belief that this man's words didn't threaten him.

The man quickly stood up. "Okay, okay. Have it your way." And he left.

Flori looked at Charlie again and thought for the first time, *He is acting normally. This is his normal now. This is a different Charlie.*

He turned from clearing the table. "I am so happy today." And he began singing songs he had learned earlier that morning.

Flori looked at Charlie and wondered, *Has he snapped? He was not annoyed by the confrontation with that successful and influential businessman. He was singing at the top of his voice. I have never seen him happier. Why have I never seen him happier?* Little comments or situations that would have agitated him now seemed to pass by unnoticed. He took her in his arms and tried to dance right in the kitchen. By the afternoon, she had a growing headache. Even a walk in the yard didn't seem to stop its advance. Before dinner, she was shivering and putting on her second sweater and heading to their room.

Charlie came down after a few hours. "We have been invited to go skiing! They are going to a ski resort several hours away next Saturday, December 21. Just for the day. I want to go."

"Charlie, I am sick. I think I have a fever. I cannot go."

"I was hoping you would feel better by then. Maybe you will be better in the morning. We will see. You might want to go."

"We are not very good skiers, Charlie. They will think we are not worth spending the money on taking us skiing."

"No, they want us to go with them. It will be fun. I hope you are better and do not miss the adventure."

Flori wondered if Charlie intended to go on the trip without her. They had been constant companions in adventures since they had first met. They did not leave one behind to go and spend the day with other people. What did this mean? A thousand fever-induced worries began to grow.

"This is a great opportunity. You may feel better and want to go with us."

CHAPTER 58

Kirkland, Washington
December 20–21, 1991
Flori

THERE IT IS. CHARLIE INTENDS to go without me. Even if I felt better, the announcement the family would be away for an entire day seemed like an opportunity for us to be alone. A day with several, long-overdue conversations, and renewed intimacy would be something to look forward to enjoying. But it is clear Charlie has changed.

"Feel better and want to go?" Charlie actually had said that to me! How little he is paying attention. Going back to sleep is a relief from thinking. Thinking hurts, just like every muscle and bone in my body hurts more each hour.

For several days, my sleep has been restless, feverish torment. The headache and night sweats continue each night until the early morning hours. Charlie gets up, and I finally fall into a more peaceful sleep pattern. Each afternoon, I hope for recovery, but by late afternoon I am once again miserably sick with the flu.

Upstairs, as the weekend nears, Charlie and the family spend hours preparing to leave for skiing. On Saturday morning before daybreak, Charlie wakes me up with grunting as he tugs on a pair of boots borrowed from a church member. Over his shoulder, Charlie explains they will return late, after dinner and after dark.

I had just fallen into the morning deep sleep pattern. However, I manage to get up and take a warm shower, which feels better than anything else has for almost a week. Drying off and slipping on a pair of pants and warm top, I climb the stairs to say goodbye. However, instead of busy chatter and preparations, there is silence. They have already left. Had he even said goodbye? I feel another wave of weakness invade my legs, and I sit down at the kitchen table. There is no note. The house is empty.

All that day, I have short periods of rest and sleep. But by evening, I am well enough to write Aunt Cristina a letter that successfully shares nothing more than weather and greetings. What can I say? Charlie is not better. We are on the West Coast with $180. Charlie seems like a totally different man. He is extremely happy—maybe too happy. Yes, he is too happy. He is obsessed with religion. I certainly cannot share that news! He doesn't talk with me about important decisions. I want a plan about such things as returning home or reuniting to be a family again. There is no plan. There is no plan to reunite with Marius. And Charlie has left his sick wife to go off and slide down a mountain on sticks.

How can I tell my family how difficult it is to be surrounded by the church families with adorable children and babies? How can I put into words how it intensifies my longing for Marius?

The pastor and his wife have an incredibly generous and kind family. They share everything with an easy attitude. It is overwhelming to receive hearty meals, a warm room and bed, and true friendship. We have nothing to give back. In Romania, we enjoyed being generous to our friends by picking up restaurant bills or offering favors. We were proud to give expensive gifts, and I think pride was a big part it. Here we are not given expensive meals, but we share everything they have. We never gave with the open and humble attitudes of our hosts. These gifts are magnified by the rare attitude in which they are given.

I don't want to read the Bible constantly like Charlie seems driven to do, but I suspect it might explain why they can be so kind. They often quote a passage of scripture when I try to thank them. It is too much to understand, much less explain in a note to either family.

I finally take a second piece of paper from the desk drawer and write out the estimated costs to return home. How could that happen with $180? I draw circles around numbers and arrows to this and to that. It still is impossible. The black and white tallies mock my plans and only show me a clearer picture of my despair. I am too ashamed to write and ask for money to buy a ticket. Crumpling the sheet, I quickly put the paper away. Charlie will be very disappointed if I write to access funds from our accounts in Romania. It certainly would alarm my family and suggest things are not as good as my previous letters had led them to believe. How international banking and money transfers work is a mystery to me. Looking out of the living room window at the bare winter trees and gray sky, I grieve that we have left Marius, and nothing is improving with Charlie. I see no plan; I feel no hope.

I am not sure how long I cry into the sofa pillow, but thousands of tears drench it to a new color. In an attempt to feel as well as I had after my morning shower, I take a second shower. I cry in the shower; I cry myself to sleep. When I cry, my nose and head hurt more with the pressure, but I continue to cry. I can't put my head down on the pillow, so I build a tower in the bed with pillows from the couch and bed. My eyes water; my ears hurt. I want every blanket, and then I kick them all off. I get up and randomly wander through the house. I go back to bed. The day is never-ending.

I want to dislike these people and this country. But all they do is act in love. They share about a God who loves them and wants to love me. I don't know a God who loves me. But I can't imagine anyone being more loving than these people. We have never known anyone who would do for us what these strangers are doing. These people act like they know a God who does love everyone.

I see my new Bible rests on Charlie's side of the bed. I reach out to touch it. A soothing calm fills me with the hope of a peaceful nap. I close my stinging eyes and rest. Waking with a memory of an evening at the home of two church members, Claudia and George and their three children, I realize I am no longer crying. Claudia and George had not heard the story of Marius's miracle, and so we shared it with them. It had moved the family to tears. They had spontaneously offered prayers of thanksgiving. Later, Claudia had simply said, "You want God to be in you. It changes the way everything looks and feels. If you want something, you will find everything you need in his book." It was a sweet memory to wake up and remember.

I see that Charlies's Bible is near me on the bed. "How can this book comfort me now? How?" My doubt echoes, repeating again and again I my heart. Randomly, I open to Luke 2:6.

"While they were there, the time came for the baby to be born. And she gave birth to her firstborn, a son. She wrapped him in swaddling cloths and placed him in a manger because there was no room for them in the inn" (NIV).

Instantly my tears flow again. "This isn't comforting! I am without my own husband and without my own baby son!" And then my rage begins to grow, spilling out between the tears. I continue to scream my anger to the empty walls, the empty house. The more I use words to describe the hurt and anger, the more quickly bitterness increases.

"Who do these people think they are that God cares about them? Do they think they are so much better than priests and saints? These people think they know so much more. Their words put me down as they puff themselves up.

"Each conversation is not in love. It is all about how wonderful they are, and how they pity us. Are room and board worth this humiliation?

"And their worship! Is it any different than 'the monkey see, monkey do' of the Orthodox service? There is no choice. They sing; they pray. They stand up; they sit down." I throw the Bible across the bed, and it falls to the floor. Upon hearing the heavy thud, I hesitate, but my hateful words now flow with power. "People, even these people, are not friends with God. People are but ants to God. Did God remember me and have our son fall into a pipe? Where was God when we needed him? I had to save my son, and now I need to save my husband! I must find a way!"

I begin to plan my own vengeful return to Romania. There is not enough money, but if I can overcome that and get money somehow to buy a ticket, I can go home. I don't care if returning by myself means I would never be able to get a return visa to the United States! I might never know what happens to Charlie after I go. I am exhausted thinking about what he needs. He isn't himself. If I leave, I will abandon him when he needs help the most. But he may never be the Charlie I married again. Maybe Marius needs me more than Charlie! Each direction I turn to solve my problems seems only to show me how much trouble I am really facing. Waves of anger I don't know exist, and the absolute darkness of aloneness, surround me.

After an hour of complete despair, I find the strength to stand up and wash my face. I look into the mirror and see the anger and pain. Dark circles under my eyes and the shape of my mouth look nothing like the soft, loving face of Marius's mother. I quickly turn off the bathroom light.

I sarcastically sing out, "God doesn't speak to me. So they must be so much better than I am." I slam the bedroom door, and it echoes through the empty house. I collapse on the bed until well after the sun sets. "Where is Charlie? Has there been an accident on the ski slopes? In the car? Why are they not home?" Tears flow again, and I curl up in the bed, wrapped and swaddled in a borrowed comforter. A choked sob escapes. "I am a mother! Who is watching over Marius like I would? Who would know him well enough even to see signs that maybe the accident in the pipe might still have some strange, unexpected consequence? He needs me! He needs me! He needs his mother!" The sobs drain all the remaining life from my chest. Until all I can do is whisper, "I need! I need my baby to be here with me."

I wait in the bedroom's frozen silence until I hear the door open and voices enter the house. I wait, rehearsing the conversation. Charlie will come in and kiss my forehead. He will regret he has left me so sick to go and ski. He will apologize, and it will be the right time to begin the necessary conversation we need to return home.

Charlie comes in and turns on the small desk lamp. I sit up, waiting for his greeting. "Oh, Flori, I had the best time!" He quickly begins unpacking and shedding the layers of borrowed ski clothes. "We had so much fun. We laughed all day. The trees were so big. We bought a souvenir, pine-tree-scented hangers for the car to remember such a great day." Then he prepares for bed and slips under the comforter. He doesn't look at me as he pats my leg. "We will tell you more about it tomorrow in the morning."

That is all. Within a few minutes, he is snoring softly. And as quickly, I start spinning through the same angry logic I had during the entire afternoon. *Why didn't he look at my face and see? Why doesn't he see my fear in my eyes? He no longer even sees me. Is this how a loving husband treats his wife?* Christianity has damaged and, in fact, aggravated his problems. It has delayed his healing, and maybe I cannot continue to hope that he will ever return to himself. Charlie is gone; he is changed.

These last two lines repeat with each beat of my heart. They pound the truth into every cell, and the weight of this idea grows, crushing my chest and reducing my breathing to a mere whisper of breath. The pain increases to an unbearable level. I feel pinned in the bed, my arms and legs too heavy to move. It is incredible work to breathe. I have to concentrate to lift my chest and bring in just a sip of air. I lie on my back, and my tears flow down my cheeks and drop onto the sheets. I am powerless even to wipe them away. They carry unspeakable pain, and my grief flows with them. I feel no one in the darkness. It seems possible just to stop breathing, to let go, and to die. Only the thought of Marius causes me to wonder if my heart's whisper might be heard.

"God, come into my heart! Or God, let me die! I was on vacation in Romania, and I was three people—my husband, my son, and me. I almost lost my baby. Now, I am in America with my husband. He is completely crazy. I cannot handle this anymore. I give up. God, come into my heart, or let me die!"

Immediately the intense pain decreases, and I can feel it retreat until I can take a deep breath. The next breath comes more easily. There is lightness within my body, and beyond that, there is light within my heart. The intense burdens have fallen away, and my arms and legs move freely. If wishing this peace to be real had been possible, I would have delivered myself—saved myself hours ago. Now, suddenly, I feel liberated and exhilarated by unspoken prayer? I test with another deep breath. How could this be so? Warmth fills where the pain was. Calm love replaces my anger. It radiates through my cells. I feel it move from my heart into each finger and toe. *Is this a dream? I don't ever want to wake up. This is better than life. Maybe I did die.*

Only feeling the wet warmth of my tears running down my neck and onto the pillow reassures me I am both alive and awake. I can wipe them away with my fingertips. These are not painful, heavy tears. These are tears full of light and giggles. I feel safe and secure, immeasurably rich and blessed. I cannot name anything that had ever been wrong or bad in my life. Thoughts of Marius make me laugh with joy. Everything will work out. In fact, everything is already being worked out better than I can see or understand. I can't think of anything I should or even could worry about.

This must be a dream. And I release myself into a deep and peaceful sleep. Several times I awake, and each time I feel the joy of my holy dream melt into a blessing of life. The wonderful feeling continues each time. I test the peace by thinking of my son, the lack of money, and even Charlie. Charlie experienced what he called "popcorn happy." I am now popcorn happy! How can this be so? A solid confidence that hope has transformed my fear grows. Without any pain, I once again fall peacefully back to sleep.

CHAPTER 59

Kirkland, Washington
December 22, 1991
Flori

WHEN I WAKE UP, CHARLIE is still sound asleep. It is Sunday, and I am still amazed how healthy and energetic I feel. I bounce out of bed into the bathroom. Looking into the mirror, I glow! I smile, and all I want to do is keep smiling and saying "thankyou" to everyone and about everything! The sound of breakfast preparations and dishes hints the pastor's wife is awake and in the kitchen.

When I reach the top of the stairs, Vio turns to greet me. "Why are you laughing downstairs? You are alone, yes?"

"Yes, I am alone although I don't feel like I am alone anymore," I say. "Let me tell you what happened to me last night. I am so happy. I prayed God would take over my life or let me die. And I didn't die!" I start giggling again although I am not sure why.

"What! You have a smile from ear to ear." Vio runs across the kitchen and hugs me. She jumps up and down and starts to cry.

"Vio, why are you crying? I cannot cry; I can only laugh. I don't understand why I feel so wonderful."

"Jesus did this for you. He did this for you. He bought his joy for you on the cross. And now you are in his light."

We hug. She cries, and I am smiling and laughing.

"It is like love is air. It is warm and surrounds me, and there is no weight of pain or fear. Nothing has changed since yesterday when my despair overwhelmed me, and yet there is no heaviness now, and I am filled with a happiness I could not create."

Vio looks at me and hugs me again. "You cannot stop smiling, Flori. You cannot keep it in. What did Charlie say?"

"Nothing, he is still asleep. Besides, until you told me, I didn't understand what had happened to me. I didn't understand, so how could I have told him? Why didn't you tell me how it would be to have Jesus in my heart? How good it would be and about this happiness?"

"I did tell you."

"I don't remember. But now I understand, but I also don't understand. How does this happen? How can it be this simple? I was so poor, and now I feel so rich!"

We begin to have a new type of conversation; it is easy. For the first time, I talk freely about Marius. The devastating sadness that had overcome me whenever I even thought of him being so far away no longer has the same smothering pain. I go on and on, enjoying, sharing with my friend about how adorable and smart Marius is. The more I share, the more I have to share.

When Charlie wakes up and comes upstairs, he immediately can see we are sharing a great secret. "What has made both of you so happy?"

"Jesus is in my heart. I asked him, and now I am crazy happy too."

Charlie covers his face with his hands and bends down low. Then he grabs me and starts jumping up and down, praising Lord Jesus. He almost knocks me off balance, so I join him jumping. "Now we are crazy together. Flori, now you understand what I cannot explain. We can be crazy together!" Charlie breaks down and sobs. He covers his face as though embarrassed, and he sits in the kitchen chair. I put my arms around him.

Twirling the curls at his forehead, I whisper, "I am sorry. I thought you were crazy, but you will not have to explain. That will not be between us. I am crazy now too." Charlie reaches out and pulls me into his lap. Then we both cry without embarrassment.

Family members hear the commotion in the kitchen, and soon they all are embracing and laughing. Within ten minutes, we head over to the church and are sharing with early-arriving members of the church. The congregation's excitement and joy surround us and multiply our delight. I explain what had happened the night before. As people hear the story, I become part of an explosion of community praise. Some raise their arms and look up with tears flowing freely. Others praise the Lord with spontaneous prayers and songs. Charlie adds his witness to the change and how only now he understands the gift of a believing wife. I am still smiling.

Later in the afternoon, I cuddle into my husband's arms. Charlie says, "Flori, I am so relieved, I do not have to find the words to explain this happiness. Now we share it."

"Everything is different now. Everything will always be different. We will be different together."

CHAPTER 60

Kirkland, Washington
Christmas 1991

CHARLIE AND FLORI'S FIRST CHRISTMAS in the United States was completely different from any they had ever had. In Romania, Christmas had been a time to have friends over and for an evening's visit. They would laugh, eat, and drink. A Christmas tree was the center of their social expression of the holiday. It had to be big and decorated with expensive glass ornaments. Each glass ball would be delicately painted with flowers and trimmed with gold filigree and ribbons at the top. No one talked about it, but the competition was fierce to outdo friends by adding more and more expensive ornaments each year. Charlie and Flori never considered going to church.

They would set the table with the best china, and small dishes of the best appetizers were served with expensive wines and liquors. Although Charlie didn't normally drink, on Christmas evening he would drink shots with his friends. The liquor was strong and would burn deep within his chest. He would shake his head and laugh. It wasn't a feeling he had enjoyed, but it was what was done at Christmas. The children would eat at a smaller table in the living room, and perhaps a hired musician or friend would play the harmonica or the accordion. They sang familiar, folk tunes from their childhood. Then they would all go out to a popular restaurant and eat an expensive dinner, not returning home until almost the next day.

Everyone had a new outfit, and, like the ornaments, they had to be formal and expensive. It was a nice holiday, but it had none of the things that they now believed were central and important. In this community of believers in America, Charlie and Flori learned many new hymns called carols because they were Christmas hymns. "Why carols? What does that mean?" No one knew. "Why not Fred? Christmas Freds!" Charlie joked.

They made special cookies, but it was more about working together and visiting than impressing each other. The women shared recipes and ingredients. They washed each other's mixing bowls and cookie pans. When the cookies crumbled, the men would come in and grab the crumbs and make happy sounds of encouragement. When a batch burned, the women sympathized and comforted the young woman.

The Christmas tree was nice, but not as big or as expensively decorated as the ones in Charlie and Flori's friends' homes. On it were hung ornaments the children had made each year at Sunday Class and other handmade decorations telling the story of the birth of Jesus. Lights twinkled and brightened the dark, winter night, and there was always Christian music, old and modern, playing nearby.

The Christmas Eve service started loudly and joyfully, with trumpets and drums and loud singing. Then Vio brought out a cake they had made earlier in the day. Flori was surprised because she had not seen Vio decorate the cake with the words "Happy Birthday, Jesus!" Everyone sang, "Happy Birthday" to Baby Jesus. And toward the end of the service, the lights were lowered, and each person held a candle and sang "Oh Holy Night", and "Oh Little Town of Bethlehem." The words were so beautiful that Charlie cried freely. When others saw him, their tears flowed freely and joyfully too.

On Christmas Eve, Charlie and Flori especially enjoyed re-reading the birth narrative in their downstairs room. Flori said, "He was a king, and yet people knew something entirely different had happened on the night he was born. But it was so simple. They lived in a barn because they did not have a place to stay. It was borrowed! Someone shared that space with them. It was so simple and humble."

"Flori, I shared the feeling of no place to go, as there had been no room for us. I understand this now. Why could I not feel it before?

I feel so for Jesus's mother. She was amazing. She followed her husband although the trip was so difficult for her. She didn't understand, but she went with him. She was so young, and she left her mother at such a time. How could she not be afraid? And I have a wife like that. And you did not know Jesus, and yet you followed me here to take care of me, even when I might have been crazy. Why did I not understand how difficult it was for you?"

Flori smiled and said, "Ahh, then they had to go to Egypt. Without much money, they left everything behind, and Joseph did what the Lord told him to do. He didn't know how it would turn out. But he did what he was told to do. Why didn't we hear this before? How come no one told us this story?"

Charlie looked seriously at the Bible in his hands. "We had one in our home."

"Yes, but it was never to read. It was to show."

"Maybe you can only understand Jesus's story when it is given to you by God to understand truly in your hearts."

They walked out into the backyard into the silence that only new snow brings to the winter nights. Charlie drew Flori closer, and they marveled at the number of stars. Charlie whispered, "I am so happy to share this with you. It is a hundred, a thousand, a million times better with you." Charlie hummed parts of a few carols, and they just held each other.

"Our first Christmas Eve in America," Flori said.

"Yes, the best one ever! The best one until we have when Marius is here!" Charlie promised. They both returned to their room shivering.

The next morning after the excitement of Christmas morning with the family's children, Flori and Charlie helped make the casserole dishes the family would share with anyone who showed up for dinner. The night before, Pastor Doru said, "Everyone is invited here to share dinner tomorrow at two. If you don't have plans, we have food and room." The children were now busy setting the tables with colorful napkins and handwritten nametags.

The celebration was sincere. There were stories and laughter and memories shared.

"What was Christmas Eve like when you were in Romania?" someone asked Charlie.

"Oh, it was different. No Lord Jesus." But that was all Charlie would say. He was ashamed so much of his Romanian Christmas that had been about showing off and being important in the eyes of his friends. He had enjoyed being important. Tonight, Charlie understood he was important to God. So all the rest seemed like such embarrassing foolishness.

They stayed up late tracing all the unexplainable chain of events that had brought them to this church in Washington, USA, and into the family of Jesus. All unexplainable events had been unexpected and sometimes unappreciated gifts. Each event could be thought of as being like an ornament to hang on a Glorious Christ Tree:

* Meeting each other,
* Adopting Marius,
* Becoming a family,
* The accident,
* The rescue,
* The trip to the hospital,
* Lady Doctor Mariana,
* Marius being raised,
* Lady Doctor Mariana,
* Finding St. Nicholas Church,
* Charlie's feeling he had to leave Romania,
* The students and travel agencies,
* The passports and visas,
* The man who exchanged their money,
* Monk Argatu,
* The kindness of a stranger on the plane who had passed on names and contact numbers of the Washington pastor,
* The kindness of a young medical student during exams,
* Finding the United Airlines ticket agency on a busy New York street,
* Getting tickets and flying to Washington—the wrong Washington that had turned out to be the perfect Washington,

* A congregation and pastor who extended extraordinary hospitality,
* Aunt Cristina and their families who adored Marius,
* The Holy Spirit,
* Jesus Christ, their Lord, and Savior.

This tree could be decorated with Lord Jesus's anonymous interventions. How easy it might have been to miss these gifts, not to notice how they all fit together. And then suddenly, God had shown them how all those events fit together. The puzzle image was of a beautiful Christ Tree, a tree planted by God's faithful pursuit of his children, and the tree of Lord Jesus's gift of eternal life.

CHAPTER 61

Kirkland, Washington
January of 1992

ONE NIGHT IN MID-JANUARY, CHARLIE and Flori took a walk before they turned in for the night. They were bundled in coats and hats, but there was no wind. The sky was dark, and yet on the horizon, a pure, blue haze faded to a peach memory of the sun. It transformed the black silhouettes of the bare tree branches into soft, velvet masterpieces. Three or four early stars appeared above. "These same stars shine above our son." Charlie kissed Flori's head. "I miss him with each breath, but I have a peace this separation is necessary for him to have the life we are meant to live. Flori, I did not think of leaving Romania, ever. But God had a different plan for us. Now I cannot think about leaving this country."

"Charlie, I understand. I do not have the words to explain why I understand, but I also know it is true. Before I had Jesus in my heart, I could not even think of Marius without having pain in my body. Now when I think about him, I am happy. I smile; I do not cry. Why is that? I trust you, but even more, I trust the Jesus in you. Now he is in me too. I say, 'Okay.'"

"Okay? Flori, all you have to say is okay?"

"Yes, no questions. I say okay. We will stay and send for Marius."

"Oh, now I know Jesus is in you. You have nothing to say, but okay!"

Flori laughed. "I am saying okay to Lord Jesus, not to you, Charlie!"

Charlie laughed. "Flori, you are a wise woman in the spirit." Charlie paused, content in the silence for several minutes. Then he continued, "When I pulled Marius up out of the pipe, I saw death in him, but I didn't see the death that was in me. You and I were dead too; we just hadn't died yet. When he came alive, I thought I had saved him.

"Now I understand differently. Our doctor said only God could do such a miracle. God saved our son, and we didn't even know how to thank Him properly. We lit a candle to say 'thankyou' only because Doctor Lady Mariana told us to go to church and say 'thank you' to God. I am so ashamed we lit a candle with so little understanding of what Lord Jesus had done. A hundred reasons could have prevented us from knowing he was even in the pipe. And he didn't breathe or have a heartbeat for over eight hours. How could we have thought we had saved Marius?"

Flori was fighting tears and just nodded and rested her head on Charlie's chest.

"Lord Jesus saved our son, but it wasn't an eternal resurrection. I now desire an eternal resurrection in Christ for Marius. We will raise our son in faith, and I am certain he will also accept Lord Jesus. We will all be baptized, and we will all have an eternal resurrection. You and I will never have that terror of death again."

"You are right, Charlie," Flori said, "Jesus will make us strong when we are weak. He will help us through the suffering without Marius. He did not save him from death in the pipe, and he didn't bring us here to receive faith and hope only to take our son now away from us. In Jesus' time, when we have grown in faith, his time will be perfect. And we will be together again." Flori waited a few minutes and then whispered, "Our family will not understand. They will think we have abandoned them—abandoned Marius."

"It will be difficult for them to understand. How can we explain all of this? We will send for our son. It might take a month or so for him to arrive, but we will send for him. We will be here together. We need to raise Marius here, surrounded by believers." Charlie held Flori a little bit closer. They stood together in the increasing dusk. Charlie began humming the limited refrains of several new songs he was learning. Just when she had thought she recognized the tune, he would begin a new one.

Feeling so safe, Flori cuddled in closer. "The morning of the accident, I thought everything was perfect. I remember clearly thinking we had everything we needed. And now it means nothing to leave all of that behind. We had nothing. Now we have Jesus."

Charlie started laughing, and it echoed in the cold, night air, filling the branches of nearby evergreen trees and distant starlight with joy. "Yes, but we have the miracle of Lord Jesus, and he is our family's everything."

Flori started laughing too. And her laughter, like musical notes, danced around Charlie's peels of booming laughter.

CHAPTER 62

August 22, 1995
Sky Harbor, Phoenix AZ

THE LOCAL TV NEWS COVERED the reunion of a five-year-old Romanian boy with his parents in Phoenix today. The young boy ran into the arms of his father and joyfully lifted his son onto his shoulders. Surrounded by friends, Charlie and Flori tearfully welcomed their son to America with balloons and prayers of thanksgiving. The family looks forward to life here in sunny Arizona.

Of course, the bigger story was left untold to the viewers that night. How could a two-minute spot at the end of the day's news tell it all? It was a day of untold and extraordinary healings. Happily, the three of them immediately adjusted to the new routine of family life. Charlie says he had expected to have to earn his son's trust and even love again. But Marius never acted as though there was anything to be forgiven. Grace was in place.

Marius never seemed to miss Romania and quickly learned English. His teachers even remarked they didn't know he could not speak English, as he followed directions and understood lessons as quickly as the other kindergarten children. He flourished in the United States. Charlie and Flori delighted in each moment: eating breakfast together, riding in the car, singing songs, and going to parks filled with other children. Everything was enormously thrilling, and all things seemed new.

It took three and a half years for Flori and Charlie to be reunited with Marius. Many do not understand how Charlie and

Flori remained in the United States without their son. It is clear the Mada's lawyers encouraged an expectation they would be reunited within a month or two. To face so many dates of disappointment is an emigrant's story. So it was a daily struggle and heartache mixed with hope. A Christian's understanding of hope is living confidently and consistently believing what has been promised has also been accomplished, even though we cannot see or experience it yet. Their faith was strengthened and matured through this period.

When they struggled, waves of peace flooded over them, and they accepted and sought this comfort. What they would have thought to be impossible was made possible.

Flori and Charlie would write and send gifts. Photographs were sent to them of Marius showing little interest in the gifts, but climbing into the box to be mailed to them in the United States. Phone calls were expensive, with long distance fees costing $60 or more for a phone call. Occasionally, a short 8mm movie would arrive, showing Marius climbing on the railings of the Promenade. The contact seemed like a lifeline, but the silence following the calls or letters or photographs seemed an even harsher emptiness. Whenever those most frustrating and unbearable moments invaded and threatened the positive thoughts, in prayer they would seek and be filled with an unexplained peace.

Flori also was reminded in the anguishing moments before Marius had been rescued and lifted from the pipe, she had said, "God, let him live. I don't want him to die, but I prefer to be separated from him than to have him die. But let him live." There was nothing in the situation suggesting any additional separation other than the one they were experiencing as they struggled to get him out of the pipe. Now she understood and accepted those words were prophetic, a deep moaning of the Holy Spirit's prayer—and her acceptance of this separation was part of living a grateful life.

Charlie would say, "What can Lord Jesus not do? We have seen his power and his love. We say, 'Your will be done.' And now we are living. 'His will be done.'"

They both were convinced Marius would come to live with them, and they lived one day at a time with prayer and hope. Aunt

Cristina faithfully cared for Marius with the support and love of both Charlie's and Flori's extended families. During this time, neither Flori nor Charlie's families understood their decision. The stories of crazy Protestant churches echoed in their wakeful nights. They wondered what kind of people Flori and Charlie had met, who now held such influence over their decision not to return home. The Madas's personal investments left behind in Romania paid for Marius's and Aunt Cristina's expenses. The Madas left behind their worldly possessions, their careers, and business.

Charlie and Flori struggled with the separation from their parents, families, and friends, but a peace ruled in their hearts. That peace and their gratitude for the miracle of their son's life and the saving grace of knowing Jesus sustained them with daily, unexpected comfort. They do not completely understand it, but they lived it. Strength and comfort were divine gifts.

The Madas also recalled the man, who insisted he only exchange money with Flori at the National Bank in Romanian before the trip, had said the strangest thing. "When you go to the United States, you will be with a group of Protestant people. You will hear about Jesus. Doesn't matter what is happening—do not depart from them." At the time, they had disregarded his words as ridiculous, but now they took them very seriously. They committed themselves always to remain in a strong community of believers who consistently lived according to the Word.

In 1992, and with the support of the friends, Flori and Charlie applied for Permanent Resident status in the United States, and with working papers and determination, they slowly began to rebuild a stable, independent, and comfortable life in Washington. They drove a truck and planned on starting a trucking company. Increasingly frustrated with their inability to get Marius to the United States, they were advised to move to Arizona where there was a more efficient immigration process.

In March of 1994, Flori and Charlie moved to Phoenix, Arizona, and within a couple of months had accomplished what their legal team in Washington could not. In December of 1994, they received Permanent Resident status in the United States.

In God's timing, all things were made right. Through their Romanian Baptist Church in Phoenix, the Madas knew of a trustworthy woman who would be traveling to Bucharest, and she agreed to bring their son back to the United States. Surprisingly, the legal procedure and paperwork to accomplish this were completed within weeks. Finally, Charlie and Flori Mada were reunited with their son at Sky Harbor Airport in Phoenix on August 22, 1995. The local TV news covered the meeting as a smiling, five-and-a-half-year-old boy rushed into his parents' arms. It was a day of days with untold, extraordinary healing.

And so Flori and Charlie pondered the many amazing miracles they witnessed, and they quietly lived lives of gratitude. It would take another eighteen years to put the mysterious pieces of these years together and see the way it really all fit together. The story of their story only seemed like another part of the mysterious miracles begun on a day next to the Danube River, when they munched on melon and foolishly thought they had everything.

AUTHOR'S NOTES

Phoenix, AZ
Ocean Grove, NJ
2013 to 2017

THE MADAS SHARED THEIR STORY with believers occasionally, but usually they told the story privately to people with whom they had developed a relationship. They were active in their church, worshiping, and studying the Bible. Then close friends and advisors began telling them they should write out the story. Their answer was always the same. "When Lord Jesus wants us to write it out, he will tell us. We will feel like we have his green light when to tell His story." The frequency of the unsolicited recommendations to write out the details continued and increased.

Charlie and Flori Mada attended Compass Bible Church in Youngtown, AZ, for about twelve years. In the spring of 2013 Charlie shared the story of Marius's accident at the morning service. He spoke for about fifteen minutes and found it very emotional. Many people in the congregation cried and encouraged them to write out the story. Again, Charlie answered, "When Lord Jesus wants us to write, he will tell us. We will feel like we have his green light when to write his story."

In their mid-week Bible study class on August 15, 2013, they were studying the book of Revelation. After class, a good friend named Frank asked Charlie, "Why did you come to the United States?" Charlie thought to repeat the familiar story of the tour group, but he hesitated. Charlie heard the question more clearly. Charlie knew

Frank was hoping for a deeper answer than the specific events and situations that had led to getting on the plane. What was the purpose of Charlie's journey to the United States?

Charlie suddenly had a new clarity. He answered, "When the accident happened, and I was in the deepest despair, I prayed directly to God. God brought us to the United States to meet with his son, Lord Jesus."

Frank's reply was simple. "You have to write the story."

There was something in Frank's words that penetrated their hearts in an entirely new way.

Without a formal discussion, Flori and Charlie both struggled with Frank's words. They accepted them as true. Both were far more confident than they had ever been. God was sending this message. However, the practical process of how to write a book was overwhelming. Later that evening, Flori prayed, "God, I don't want this to be my thought, but yours. Send me a sign. If you want us to write a book, then send us an author."

"Charlie, I realized that when I pray to Lord Jesus, I prayed all the words in the Romanian language. But the word author was in English! I immediately understood that the book will be in English! How do we write a book in English? We need an author! We don't know anyone to write in English." She decided to wait, certain that God would provide a clear sign.

The next Sunday morning, August 18, 2013, the Phoenix Romanian Baptist Church leader, Octavian, was visiting with Compass Bible Church and waved and greeted Flori and Charlie. He persisted, "You must write the story of what God has done for you through Jesus. Do not hide your light under a basket. Hearing your story might encourage someone to want to get to know Jesus better. Look in the Bible. Why does Jesus heal or raise the dead?"

During the cafe fellowship between Sunday class and worship, three separate people approached Flori and Charlie to encourage them to write their miracle story. They gave each the same reply. "God will have to tell us. I can be patient for God. He is patient with me." This increased frequency of unsought advice upset Flori because she did not want people to push God's timing. She went into the sanctuary and sat down in the pew. "How are we going to write a book in English?"

Although I live in New Jersey, I was in the Phoenix area visiting my family that same Sunday. I had attended services at Compass Bible Church several times and had found the congregation very friendly. When I came into the church, I was looking for the Madas. I had met the attractive and outgoing couple before and had heard their miraculous story from my sister, Kathe; but on this occasion, I had a specific reason for seeking them out. I wanted to ask if they had a written account of their story to send to my son, Dan.

Several months earlier, as he and I drove along the Pan-American Highway in Panama, Central America, I had tried to express my concerns about several things near Rio Mission Base where he and his wife, Jessica, served as directors. In light of Marius's story, the drainage ditches that were partly exposed seemed potentially dangerous for my grandchildren. I had several terrifying dreams about such a crisis, and I couldn't ignore the reoccurring warnings. I retold the Mada's story to convince Dan to take precautions and explained my fears were intensely attached to the Mada story. He asked if they had written an account of the events. "They should," he looked over and smiled. "I would like to read it."

Four months after that conversation with our son, and unaware of the morning's other three inquiries from church members about a written account of Marius's miracle, I found Charlie and Mada after the service. "Do you have a written account of your son's accident? The whole story? My son is interested in reading it."

Flori did not smile, but looked at me very seriously and simply said they did not.

Rather impulsively, I replied, "Well, I am a writer, and if I can ever help you do that, I would be honored."

Overwhelmed, Flori had sat down and cried. I looked at her and wondered what I had said that had offended her and would make her cry. I looked at her, and then to Charlie, and I am sure he saw my confusion as to what to do next. Again, I was uncertain if I should comfort her.

Charlie grabbed me and hugged me. "You are an answer to prayer," he said.

But even then, I did not know what an immediate and timely answer to prayer the offer had been. I remained confused and a bit concerned about Flori's reaction. Flori quickly got up and gave me a huge, long hug.

She explained to me, "When I prayed to Lord Jesus about this book, I prayed in the Romanian language, but the word author came out in English. So I know that the book should be written in English. When do you want to start?"

Long journeys begin with the first step, and within two hours, I was walking a hundred yards from my mother's home to the Mada's. Sitting in their dining room, Flori brought out lots of warm and rich desserts. I enjoyed their hospitality as they began to tell me their story with clarity, passion, and an obsession with the accuracy of minor details. They cried and acted out major parts of the events, their English rich with a Romanian accent. They became very emotional as they actually relived the events. At times, they would search for words and fall into a rush of Romanian and ask questions to clarify English words. It was clear they had never told this story with the expanded details my questions requested. Those first three meetings each lasted over three hours. Through their hearts, the story flowed into my heart. Later in New Jersey, looking over the pages and pages of notes, the words and passion flowed out through my fingers to the keyboard and page.

In March of 2014, during a visit to Arizona, we met for additional, long, emotional sessions. Again, they poured out their hearts, and it all seemed like events they were truly reliving. It was once again a privilege on Sunday to worship with my sister and her husband and the Madas. I came in just before the hour and slipped into a pew in the back. A good-looking young man came into the service and sat down between Charlie and Flori. Suddenly, I realized the little boy I was writing about had grown into an impressive young man. This time, I was the one who sat down and cried!

Over the next year and a half, I flew to Arizona, and we would follow the same pattern around their dining room table. They would consider my various questions and say, "We didn't think about that. At the moment, we were not thinking." Other times they could answer with incredibly detailed and accurate information. More than twenty years had passed, but for them, it was still a present-tense experience. We met and worked on the project together over fifteen times during the next two years. We would follow the visits with phone calls and emails to review, and correct, or discuss details. Finally, we exchanged FedEx printed copies and email attachments.

That first morning in church, Flori insisted I used the word *author*, and although it would have been unusual for me to use, I might have. Perhaps the translation between author and writer, or the inspiration of the Spirit, transcended the difference. So many events followed, giving us each confirmation our collaboration was destined. I initially thought this project meant writing a ten to a fifteen-page essay, and I easily volunteered for that effort. It has been a life-blessing to see what has grown from offering to do what I could, and then understanding what, with Christ's guidance, I could actually accomplish.

In November of 2015, my husband and I flew out to have one final interview, and more importantly, to celebrate the Christian marriage of Marius and Kaitlin. With warm breezes and the sunset creating a classic, desert evening, the couple stood and repeated their Christian vows and exchanged rings. Could anything be more beautiful and hopeful? I felt the joy of completing the story about Marius's miracle on the such a significant day of his life.

In the introduction, I shared we were in prayer for Caroline's complete healing following her accident. On March 30, 2015, Caroline received the miracle of eternal life. Her family and the community were devastated by her sudden death. The waves of loss and grief still are overwhelming. We do not expect that to change for some time. Her spirit and love and joy will be forever missed. And yet in the middle of this unspeakable pain, the strength her parents have experienced is also unimaginable.

They returned to their home after their last goodbye at the hospital and felt a peace that could be nothing but a gift. Caroline's words as she left their home the day of the accident, "Love you more!" echoes in their hearts. They know they will give their children a happy home filled with that love. Sorrow will visit, but it will not live there.

And Caroline, who was an amazing musician, gave over twenty families their own miracles. As a high school student, she had played the violin at the dedication of the Zan's Garden of Life at Jersey Shore University Medical Center. It is a garden in memory of a doctor's daughter who had died in an automobile accident while on vacation. Her family had donated her organs, and the garden is dedicated as a quiet place of thanksgiving. Caroline had expressed her admiration at the donor's courage. Her mother said, "Sometimes the right thing to do is the most difficult thing to do." Caroline had agreed and sealed it with a hug. Caroline's family dared to share, knowing it was her wish too.

Months later, I shared this story with Kate and Bill. We discussed Marius's words: "If it happens again, don't cry because I don't want to come back."

Kate said, "That is interesting because I have wondered about that. I don't think Caroline would want to leave someplace she felt was both beautiful and comfortable. She had her opinions." We all laughed; she did have her opinions. And in some small ways, grief began transforming. Exactly what grief feels like depends on the day, hour, and moment, but eventually, comfort arrives in either some small way or in some unmistakable, more mysterious way.

Within two years, Kate's mother, Judy, also died. She had been in a coma for almost twenty-four hours when she suddenly reached up and broke into a wonderful, sweet smile. And then she took one breath and was gone. Kate knows where she has gone, and she understands the reason for the smile. Daily, Kate and Bill find the courage to carry on in blessed assurance.

A miracle, by definition, is an event or an outcome, considered extremely rare and defying rational explanations. Charlie, Flori, and Marius Mada received a true and witnessed miracle. They live in a state of extraordinary gratitude for something they did not deserve. They are grateful, not only for a temporary miracle of Marius's being raised from the dead, but also for the sure hope through Jesus Christ's promise to all believers that everyone can experience an eternal resurrection. Christ's sacrificial gift means one day, each of us can be raised!

Flori and Charlie Mada
Wedding Day, 1982
Romania

Marius at sixteen months
August 24,1991
Romania

Charlie, Marius, and Flori
18 days after the accident
Bucharest, Romania
August 24, 1991

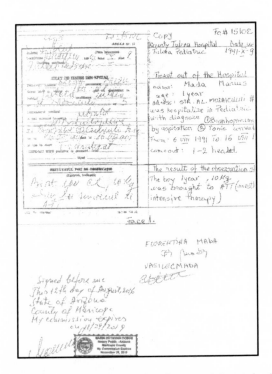

Discharge from Tulcea Hospital indicating Marius had died.
Translation authenticated

Definition for Coma IV in Romanian Medical Text 1991
Translation authenticated

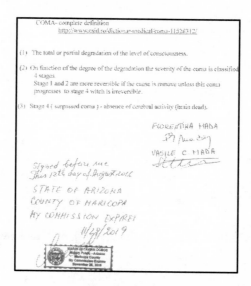

To view hospital documentation, visit www.raised.today.

Medical dispensary sector 3

Name: MADA
First name: MARIUS
Age: 16 April 1990
Adress: Mozaicului #3

DIAGNOSIS:

Delay in language development

(in 1991 – coma stge $\overline{IV}$ (1) with convulsion

The child to be observed and treated

Data:
16 Octomber ($\overline{x}$) 1991

FLORENTINA MADA

VASILE C MADA

Signed before me
This 12th day of August
State of Arizona
County of Maricopa
My commission expires

Release from Specialist after returning to Bucharest.
Translation authenticated

RAISED!

Signed before me
This 12th day of August, 2016
State of Arizona
County of Maricopa
My commission expires

Sirbu Ernest Edmond
Tulcea, Podgoriilor, no.5, bl.2, Sc A, Ap.1 - Romania

Declaration

The Undersigned Sirbu Ernest Edmond I declare the following:

On August 6, 1991, I was witness to the tragic events of the Mada family after the accident to their child Marius at the age of 16 months ; after the drowning of the child who fell into the uncovered, agriculture, irrigation tube, in the Danube Delta, Murigiol village, Tulcea County, more exactly to the shore of a lake known under the name Ghiolul Pietrei.

My relation with the family Mada: I am Flori Mada's first cousin.

On August 6, 1991 I was summoned to the Tulcea County Hospital by telephone from the Mada family where I saw Marius in the recovery room with an oxygen mask on his face.
When I touched him he was cold and stiff and of a repulsive color yellow-gray of the body. I immediately understood from my observations and as well from the discussions with the doctors that he did not have vital signs. The doctors who had examined him repeatedly said ."We do not find any sign of life within child".
In reality Marius was dead but doctors had left the child in his hospital bed in order to give time to the parents to accept the tragedy of separation of their sole child.
I was there when the doctor Maria Coman said very clearly that "they can not do anything only God can if he make it a miracle".
I got intervention with the specialist doctor for children- doctor Elena Bretcan, which was also my neighbor on the apartment building.
The doctor Elena Bretcan after personally examining Marius said ,"There is nothing that can be done. the parents should UNDERSTAND". However the doctors agreed to leave the baby in the hospital room in bed and have him watched in the hope expressed,"Maybe God will do a miracle".
In the afternoon of August 6 1991, I went together with Vasile-Charlie to the hotel Pelican in Murighiol, to bring the suitcases with things and to break the contract with the hotel for holiday because of the accident.
We stopped at the scene of the accident where it happened. Charlie showed me the pipe in which Marius had fallen. I could not believe that this was the pipe, it was small in size. When some of the people saw Vasile-Charlie Mada coming, many more people from the tents on the bank of the water who had seen when Marius drowned came to sympathize with him and to help him to gather the fishing gear which they had left on the banks of the lake.
They were witnesses of the accident.
Charlie said that Marius was at the hospital. They were amazed because they saw the DEAD toddler. They showed me the same pipe, they saw how his parents took him out of it. They said, "We would not believe the mother of the child when she told us that Marius is inside of the pipe, so we searched for him and we saw how he was taken out and what the child looked like."

FLORENTINA MADA   VASILE C MADA   Page 1

257

Some of them were are not able to look at the deformed child, others left and many of them were convinced that he was dead.

More than that I heard a big lady say to her husband, "the child drowned and I saw him when they took him out of the pipe with water, and there is no chances to be alive". She continued to explain so as her husband and a few other people who were close by could understand it was not possible for child to be alive, because he was breathless when he was removed from the tube with water, and the way to the hospital took very much time, it would have taken the ambulance at least 45-50 minutes to reach them.

Then we got back to the hospital around 9-9:30 pm where Marius and Flori were in the same room. Marius no longer had the oxygen mask on.

The doctors said, "there is no sign of life in the child but the parents don't want to accept it and we will give time to the parents, but we will have to move the child....".

I went home and the parents remained in the hospital with steady hope that Marius will live.

After midnight Charlie came to us at home with the wonderful news, "Marius LIVES'.

It was amazing to see Marius on the next day the same child as before the accident. The doctors said they do not have scientific explanation only that it is a MIRACLE.

Not only that he came back to life but it is amazing he has no physiological result caused from the accident .

Flori and Charlie were for the following 12 days together with my family, my wife Ioana Sirbu and my mother Ioana Sirbu (Aunt Cristina for Mada family).

On 18 August 1991 Charlie, Flori and Marius returned in Bucharest to their residence at that time.

The declared things are true as I have described and sign for this.

Sirbu Ernest Edmond Date
    22, July 201 6

FLORENTINA MADA

For Mada

VASILE C MADA

Signed before me This 12th day of August, 2016 State of Arizona County of Maricopa My commission expires on 11/29/2019

MARIN OCTAVIAN DOBOS
Notary Public - Arizona
Maricopa County
My Commission Expires
November 29, 2019

Page 2

Witness letter from Flori's cousin, a lawyer in Romania.
Translation authenticated

In the afternoon of the day August 6, 1991, I receive a desperate phone call from my nephews, making the announcement that they were at the hospital at Tulcea. Marius was submerged. Together with my son we left immediately to go as fast as possible to help them. From the hospital, I my son with the father of the child returned to get the lady doctor Bretan the chief leader of pediatrics, she was leaving on the second level of the apartment building where I live. When she came she immediately went to the specific room, she took information and did a physical exam of the case and she came and communicated to us " Presently nothing can be done for him, I doubled checked, only the power of God can help." And she looked up.

I know that for eight hours he was dead. There were two nurses in charge of supervising at all times. I stayed in the hallway until sunset, and my son with the father of the child went for all the baggage left in the field at this time.

(They came in Tulcea bare feet) The father of the child told me to go home, for now he is here. I went home. I got home, the phone rang and his parents gladly told me that the child came to life.

Big emotions and stress were even to the next day.

After discharge they stayed a day with us and then they all three went home to Bucharest.

In the month of November 1991, I was called by my niece to help with the child as they had to go to America. I was retired for one year and wanted to help her, and in particular because they wanted the child very much.

This child had been left in the care of me and under the protection of the parents from Dec 2, 1991 until August 1995. In this period the child was attended by all the attention of parents sending packages and the money needed for his care. On his birthday we made and sent them videos tapes.

This is my statement that I give it and I sign.

I am sending a copy of the ID for identification.

Signature – Sirbu Ioana

FLORENTINA MADA

VASILE C MADA

Signed before me
This 12th day of August 2016
State of Arizona
County of Maricopa
My commission expires
on 11/29/2019

MARIN OCTAVIAN DOBOS
Notary Public · Arizona
Maricopa County
My Commission Expires
November 29, 2019

Witness letter by Flori's aunt.
Translation authenticated

Charlie, Marius, and Flori Mada
Wedding in Arizona
November 2015

Kaitlin and Marius Mada
Wedding Day in Arizona
November 8, 2015

RAISED!

Flori, Margaret Cotton (author), and Charlie
Arizona 2015

Caroline playing violin in
Zan's Garden of Life 2013
Jersey Shore University Medical Center
Hackensack Meridian Health

GRATITUDE

WORDS CANNOT EXPRESS MY GRATITUDE for the privilege of writing Charlie, Flori, and Marius's story. Hearing and writing their story gave me an even greater understanding of Jesus's abundant provision. St. David, my husband, spent hours and hours encouraging, editing, listening and cooking when I was absorbed in writing. Flori and Charlie also spent countless hours sharing, clarifying, reading, and collaborating. They were demanding of precise wording in all quotes, the timeline, and the re-telling of their vivid memory of events and emotions. They patiently considered my countless questions and also allowed my informed and inspired imagination to fill in contextual details. The task grew from what I had thought was going to be a long essay to this book, and many times their enthusiasm and encouragement renewed my confidence.

There are many people to thank. My sister, Kathe, and her husband, Jerry, first shared the Madas' story and then shared the Madas as friends. My mother, Margaret Manson, always offered her love, prayers and encouragement. Others provided the right balance of praise, edits, and suggestions: Laura R., Debbie D., Sheree M., and my Manasquan High School girlfriends—Debbie, Sue, Lyn, Susan, Cindy, Bobbi, and Sandee—kept me laughing and reading while I was trying to write.

Marius and Kaitlin's letters to me after they read the story for the first time also deeply touched my heart. Manasquan Presbyterian Church's small group, who read an early draft, and the Prayer Intercessory Group's excitement were inspirational for me. Many thanks to Ocean Grove Camp Meeting Association for hosting an evening with the Madas, which resulted in the final rewrite of the book's format. Frank and Pat, along with Donna and Ralph, provided additional suggestions and support to the Madas in Arizona. Special thanks to Kate and Bill who, for eighteen years, shared their daughter, Caroline, and allowed me to weave their journey of faith, grace and courage into this book.

My wonderful family: our son, Daniel, with Jess and Maddie, Selah, Micah, and Emmy, and our daughter, Allison, with Paul and Adam, Luke, and Thomas, provided the blessed diversion of happy times together. The vibrant joy of our children's families helped to ground this story in the small details of life that might go unnoticed if they were not really so essential. To watch our children and grandchildren walk in Christ's light is an unimaginable blessing.

But it is the author of the miracle, Lord Jesus, to whom we are most entirely and eternally grateful.

Amen.

For small-group Bible study and discussion materials or to arrange speaking engagements, please contact Charlie and Flori Mada and Margaret J Cotton through our website Raised.today

Like and share us on Facebook- Raised@cottonmada

ABOUT THE AUTHOR

MARGARET JOANNE COTTON WAS BORN and raised at the Jersey Shore. She graduated from Kent State University and loved teaching in Jessamine County, Kentucky, and Howell, New Jersey. She wrote grants and developed curriculum for reading comprehension and writing skills, giving workshops from local school districts to state conferences. She was awarded a National Endowment for the Humanities scholarship for independent study of the religious activities of Colonial New England women. The remarkable circumstances of her meeting Charlie and Flori Mada, who live in Arizona, and then writing the Madas' story are further blessings in the cascade of miracles surrounding Raised!.

Margaret and her husband David, a Presbyterian minister, live in Ocean Grove, NJ. Their days are filled with the joys of being grandparents to seven. Their daughter, Allison with her husband and three sons live nearby, providing a rich family routine. Their son, Dan with his wife and four children, direct a Christian mission base and foundation in Central America. Summer reunions provide plenty of family beach time! Margaret is also a professional photographer who has shot over two hundred weddings. She believed from a young age her life's song is to reassure and to encourage. Telling stories of love and commitment, in text and light, is one way she serves Christ. Writing *Raised!* has been a deeply moving, humbling, and joyful highlight of her life of faith.

CPSIA information can be obtained
at www.ICGtesting.com
Printed in the USA
FFOW02n0459040618
46991017-49261FF

9 781642 581232